NEVER HOLD AN UNDERDOG DOWN

YOU ME
AT SIX

NEIL DANIELS

Published in 2012 by
INDEPENDENT MUSIC PRESS
Independent Music Press is an imprint of I.M. P. Publishing Limited
This Work is Copyright © I. M. P. Publishing Ltd 2012

You Me At Six – Never Hold An Underdog Down
by Neil Daniels

British Library Cataloguing-in-Publication Data.
A catalogue for this book is available from The British Library.
ISBN: 978-1-906191-23-8
Cover Design by Fresh Lemon.
Cover photography courtesy of Ray Tang/Rex Features

Independent Music Press
P.O. Box 69,
Church Stretton, Shropshire
SY6 6WZ
Visit us on the web at: www.impbooks.com
For a free catalogue, e-mail us at: info@impbooks.com

You Me At Six

Never Hold An Underdog Down

by Neil Daniels

Independent Music Press

CONTENTS

INTRODUCTION

Since forming in Surrey in 2004, You Me At Six have become one of the most revered and popular alternative rock bands of their generation. Three influential and critically acclaimed albums have proved that behind their famously hard-working reputation lies a very creative and modern British band. At a time when many British rock fans are looking across the Atlantic to the United States for inventive alternative rock, You Me At Six prove that there is a still a wealth of home-grown talent being nurtured in a country that has a long history of spawning legendary rock bands, right back to the days of the Stones and The Who.

However, despite their considerable successes and large, dedicated fanbase, You Me At Six haven't always been warmly received by critics. Their younger fanbase has inevitably meant they are scorned by some highbrow music journalists and seasoned rock and punk fans. Undeterred, the band plough on with their grandiose ambitions – having toured extensively around Europe and also in North America and elsewhere, You Me At Six are also one of rock's most exhilarating live bands. And their strict work ethic and innovative music has gained them a loyal following that goes beyond the word "cult".

There have also been debates about definition – that odd journalistic drive to categorise bands for convenience, even though the acts themselves rarely even think about such terminology. You Me At Six have either been lumped into the pop-punk genre or the alt-rock genre; they join Wheatus, Jimmy Eat World, Green Day, Blink-182 and Bowling For Soup in this unwanted debate. Yet as time has progressed, many observers have begun to see them perhaps more accurately as the UK's answer to the Foo Fighters.

This biography charts the rise of the Surrey band, the stories behind the making of their albums, their energetic stage performances and their eclectic range of influences. What makes this band tick and why they have become such an iconic group in a relatively short period of time? The fact that *Kerrang!* magazine nominated them for 'Best British Band' in 2008, 2009 and 2010 suggested that they were one of a kind. Finally lifting the trophy in 2011 and then again in 2012 confirmed that suspicion. Here's how they made it happen.

Neil Daniels
www.neildaniels.com
www.neildanielsbooks.wordpress.com

IN THE BEGINNING

THE FORMATION OF THE BAND

"We made an agreement that we weren't going to write any songs for anybody else."
Josh Franceschi speaking to *NME*

The very affluent and leafy town of Weybridge in Surrey, England was once the adopted home of Liverpudlians John Lennon and Ringo Starr. You Me At Six was formed there in 2004. Josh Franceschi and guitarist Max Helyer had been in a band together at school with some fellow music-loving friends but as with the majority of teenage outfits, the line-up quickly fell apart. Helyer had wanted to play the guitar for about four years before he finally got one after pestering his parents. His sister played the piano so there was already a musical vibe in the Helyer household. Helyer was a huge fan of Nirvana's tormented late guitarist/singer Kurt Cobain and wanted to write his own songs as well as play the guitar, just like Cobain. Helyer took some guitar lessons and began dedicating himself to the instrument he'd spent years nagging his parents to buy. As time progressed he became more confident and developed his own style of playing. Helyer was not only a fan of Nirvana, whose groundbreaking album *Nevermind* has influenced an entire generation of bands, but as the months ticked by he also started to dig music by such bands as Incubus and Thrice.

Helyer knew from the get-go that learning to play guitar was not going to be an easy ride. Without question the most difficult part, as he confessed to *Baeble Music*, was that "when you pick up guitar, you gotta listen to the sound and if things *sound* right ..."

Helyer shared common musical tastes with his good friend Franceschi; Josh's first ever gig had been at Wembley Arena when he was only twelve, to see his favourite band of the time, Linkin Park (with Welsh rockers Lostprophets as support). Linkin Park was formed in 1996 in California and released their multi-million selling debut album *Hybrid Theory* in 2000. The band found themselves part of the popular albeit short-lived and oft-derided nu-metal movement, a style of music that merged rap and hip-hop with metal. Linkin Park became one of the biggest bands of the Noughties following up their debut with *Meteora* in 2003, a couple of remix albums (*Reanimation* in 2002 and the Jay-Z collaboration *Collision Course* in 2004) *Minutes To Midnight* in 2007 and *A Thousand Suns* in 2010. With fifty million albums sold, Linkin Park released their fifth studio album *Living Things* in 2012. It hit Number 1 in the *Billboard* charts and received some of the best reviews of the band's career.

Josh Franceschi
Photo courtesy of Hugh Thompson/Rex Features

Of all the alternative rock and metal bands to emerge from the 1990s to find great success the following decade, Linkin Park are surely one of the most popular and iconic. They had a significant impact on You Me At Six, not least because when Josh had first picked up a guitar aged eleven he constantly practiced Linkin Park riffs whilst listening to their records.

He also soon discovered bands like The Early November and their singer, Ace Enders, and his widening tastes in music rapidly began to broaden his creative horizons. It was because of The Early November that he also started writing songs. The New Jersey rock band's debut *The Room's Too Cold* (2003) won rave reviews from critics for its alternative edge, pop punk texture and introspective, personalised lyrics which were a great influence on You Me At Six when they started out. When Josh began penning lyrics, a rather more surprising early influence was the ever-controversial rapper Eminem whom Franceschi thought was a superlative, insightful lyricist. Josh had grown up listening to his sister's self-composed songs so the concept of creating your own music was certainly not alien in his childhood household. Most songwriters are influenced by their own experience and events around them that shape their lives and as time progressed Josh would become a far more experienced and knowledgeable songwriter. "I did [English] in Secondary School and got a B," he told Scott Williams of *eGigs*. "Then I did politics, history, and film studies at college and got an A, B, C in that.

Max Helyer
Photo courtesy of Hugh Thompson/Rex Features

I hopefully can construct a sentence the majority of the time."

It wasn't long before Franceschi started thinking about forming a band and singing himself. After a few months of jamming together, Franceschi and Helyer hooked up with local bassist Matt Barnes, who was also at Brooklands College where they all studied. Franceschi was also aware of Barnes from the local rock scene and along with Helyer, the three of them set about forming a band. Barnes lived in the same street as a guitarist named Chris Miller whom they soon asked to join the band, along with drummer Joe Phillips. The school friends had played around with other members sporadically but this group was the first reasonably stable line-up, cemented in the middle of 2007. "We started this band just to party, play gigs and have a laugh really," Miller explained to Simon Rushworth of *Rush On Rock* in 2010. "It started getting more serious and we started to get more into our instruments."

With the confidence of youth, they started to write original songs, rehearse relentlessly, and began to play as many live shows as they could book. A lot of bands usually start by playing cover versions and imitating their musical heroes before they gain enough confidence to start writing and playing their own material. Their set-lists in the early days were short and mostly consisted of original material but they did play the odd cover version such as Fall Out Boy's 'Sugar, We're Goin' Down' and later on, even 'Poker Face' by Lady Gaga.

Where did the name You Me At Six come from? In their social circles at high school, they'd often used the term, "You me at..." with whatever time they'd arranged to meet a friend. This phrase stuck and so for their first ever show they put You Me At Six on the flyer ... and never changed it (another story suggests that Franceschi was on-line chatting to some girls on MSN and said "you me at six").

Fast-forward to 2012 and Josh Franceschi was asked about the band's moniker by blogger Darryl

Matt Barnes
Photo courtesy of
Hugh Thompson/Rex Features

Smyers of the *Dallas Observer*: "At the time we thought up the name, we thought we were being clever and ahead of our time… We didn't want a name that mentioned death or pianos or something fucking stupid. We wanted a name where you couldn't guess the genre."

You Me At Six also knew that it was very important to tour as much as possible in order to build up a fanbase of their own. In these very early days, they

Chris Miller
Photo courtesy of Hugh Thompson/Rex Features

would book shows based on the level of screams they'd attracted from the crowds they played to. The band's local music scene was generally quite heavy, so You Me At Six had to work even more to get the crowds on their side. Early attendance figures varied from gig to gig. If they didn't get the screams from the crowds they'd find it difficult booking the next shows. However, given how many shows they played in the early days it wasn't long before they'd acquired a favourable, albeit very modest reputation on the local live circuit.

As the band started to develop, the non-stop gigging and rehearsing obviously impacted on their personal lives. Before the band, it was all about education and the typical vagaries of teenage life such as partying, hanging out with friends and so on; You Me At Six changed all that. Although some of the members were still at college, You Me At Six was already their number one priority. Even as early as this, there was an assured confidence about the band; despite, or maybe because of their youth, they were convinced they had what it took to succeed. They just needed to enhance their talent, which they did by three or even four block sessions a week of solid rehearsals. They wanted to challenge themselves as individual musicians as much as they

"If they didn't get the screams from the crowds they'd find it difficult booking the next shows."

challenged themselves as a band unit. As soon as they'd nail one song they'd move on to the next and so on. They'd not only rehearse as a collective but each member would spend hours at home practising on their own instrument. That famous You Me At Six drive and ambition was visible right from the very start.

Max Helyer later reflected on the band's energetic beginnings when he spoke to Lewis Corner of *Digital Spy* in 2011, in the context of TV talent shows: "It just winds me up that there are a lot of decent talented people in this music industry who are not getting recognised," he stated. "There's too much time being spent on the machine. We were sixteen years old when we did our first tour; travelling by Megabus and carrying all our gear. We stayed in the shittiest, dingiest places possible because we enjoyed doing music."

Even by this stage the band already had enough original material written to compile a debut record. Funded from the money they made at their gigs, *We Know What It Means To Be Alone* was self-released on January, 1, 2007 and sold at the band's live appearances. Already they were starting to attract a following that was eager to buy their music. This included the tracks 'Promise, Promise', 'New Jersey', 'This Turbulence Is Beautiful', 'Taste' and 'The Liar And The Lighter'. At this very formative stage, there were distinctive early stylings already evident, perhaps reminiscent of such American bands as Paramore, The Academy Is… and Fueled By Ramen. You Me At Six were aiming for big crunchy choruses, deceptively simple riffs and catchy lyrics.

Armed with this EP, the band started to play yet more live shows and it's at this point in 2007 when they began to make a wider name for themselves as a prodigiously hard-working, touring band. "From the age of fifteen or sixteen we were out there playing shows throughout the country and just travelling around," Chris Miller admitted to Conor Scrivener of *SCAN* in 2011. "It takes a lot of hard work and dedication before someone finally notices you."

They were learning the tricks of the rock music trade the old-fashioned way by travelling to gigs via long trips on Megabuses or Happy Shopper buses, or sometimes courtesy of disjointed, endless train journeys. These gigs were often organised via MySpace which at the time was a new and innovative social forum that proved integral in helping the band promote their music and build up a fanbase (as with thousands of other early adopters of the site). The band lived off cheap food while any money they made from gigs went right back into the group's funds to pay for fuel, transport costs and squalid hotel rooms.

The band focused their attention on playing live shows around their local area in Surrey and parts of London. On April 10, they performed at the Camden Underworld as headliners of a bill that included other up and coming bands, namely, First Signs Of Frost, Sinfonia and From Grace. Due to constant touring and the power of MySpace, You Me At Six got the chance to support Saosin at Leeds Cockpit on May 3. Such was the excellence of their performances that they were written about in *Kerrang!* and *NME* and were offered the opening slot at the Slam Dunk Festival on Sunday, May 27, 2007. You Me At Six were the opening band at this festival at Leeds University Refectory. This was a major coup for the band; not only would they get to mingle with other bands of their ilk but they were given the opportunity to build up a fanbase outside of their own regional rock scene. The bill also included Beat Union, Failsafe, Sonic Boom Six, Mad Caddies, Paramore and Reel Big Fish. Certainly playing at the Slam Dunk Festival helped raise the band's profile, as it would with any band in the alternative scene. "I was just enjoying the shows," Max Helyer said to Steve O'Gallagher of *Push To Fire* about the band's growing reputation. "I think all of us were. We weren't really worried about how the stuff was coming out. If people don't like it, they don't like it. I mean, this is our band, this is what we like to do. We didn't really put pressure on ourselves when we started the band, we just made sure that when we went out as the first band on that we did our best and that we were remembered by the end of the night."

Due to their heavily reviewed support slot to Saosin and their Slam Dunk Festival appearance too, the band won a support slot with Paramore on June 10 at the Colchester Arts Centre. Further supports followed, including Furthest Drive at the 500 capacity Camden Underworld on June 28 and in July they supported Tonight Is Goodbye on a summer tour that also included Death Can Dance. July also saw the band featured in *Kerrang!*'s new music section. Other high-profile support slots followed such as Fightstar in September and Elliot Minor in October. They also played a headlining Halloween show at the Kingston Peel with support bands Consort With Romeo and We Have A Getaway. They grew up quickly on tour and they were learning a lot about life during their experiences on the road.

"If people don't like it, they don't like it. I mean, this is our band, this is what we like to do."

The band also soon released *Untitled*, a second independent EP in 2007, containing the tracks 'The Rumour', 'Gossip', 'Noises' and 'This Turbulence Is Beautiful'. Yet more gigs followed as did an ever-expanding range of musical influences. The obvious preference for bands such as Jimmy Eat World, Taking Back Sunday, Incubus and Thrice was something they were unashamedly proud of. Another major source of inspiration for the young band was Blink-182. Founded in 1992 as simply Blink before eventually becoming Blink-182 in 1994 with the emergence of their debut album, *Cheshire Cat*, this power trio's second album *Dude Ranch* (1997) sold over a million copies, but it was the subsequent *Enema Of The State* in 1999 and 2001's *Take Off Your Pants And Jacket* that propelled the Californian band into the mainstream consciousness with a particularly quirky American brand of pop-punk. Blink-182 continue to be one of the most influential alternative bands in the music industry, having inspired a plethora of bands, including, but not limited to Paramore, Fall Out Boy, Panic! At The Disco, New Found Glory, Motion City Soundtrack, We The Kings, Good Charlotte, Yellowcard and All Time Low.

Yet there was more to this band's CD collection than US pop-punk and alternative rock: "We listen to old school music as well," Helyer told *Baeble Music*, "like personally I'd say The Police as well, Matt would say Bob Marley, Queen." Led Zeppelin and Pink Floyd were also bands that some members of You Me At Six enjoyed listening to from time to time. There are certainly obvious alternative sides to the

"There was more to this band's CD collection than US pop-punk and alternative rock."

aforementioned bands which clearly inspired members of You Me At Six. Queen's unwillingness to stick to a chosen style of music or Pink Floyd's often bizarre leftfield progressive rock, Led Zeppelin's lengthy onstage improvisations and The Police's reggae-tinged rock are of interest to any young band that does not want to follow an agenda laid out by the contemporary trends in music. You Me At Six hungrily devoured rock's history as they trundled around the UK on buses and trains and in cars stuffed with equipment.

It was around this point in the relatively early stages of the band's career that drummer Joe Phillips and the band parted ways prior to the release of what would be their full-length debut studio album, due to differences about the future of the band and the direction of their music. His place was taken by Dan Flint who'd been playing drums for around seven years before joining the band. During high school, Flint had joined a music program and his parents bought him his first drum kit at an early age, so by the time he went to college he was a very proficient drummer.

"As I went to college with the guys, it was a music college so obviously they'd seen me play," Flint reflected during an interview with *Mike Dolbear DRUMS* in 2009. "They asked me if I could session for a tour that they were doing in the summer and then at the end of it they asked if I wanted to join … I had already paid for the first year's tuition fees at Uni [AMC in Guildford] but I thought I'd join the band and see how it goes as it's a once in a lifetime opportunity ... it was going in the right direction, so I thought I might as well take a chance." The new drummer finalised the definitive line-up of You Me At Six: John Franceschi on lead vocals, rhythm guitarist Max Helyer, lead guitarist Chris Miller, bassist Matt Barnes and Dan Flint on drums.

Despite their young years, You Me At Six remained convinced that they had the potential to succeed in the music industry, especially at a time when the music business was going through unprecedented turmoil largely due to the slump in CD sales and the increase of both legal and illegal downloads. Fuelled by this self-belief, You Me At Six continued working incredibly hard to spread the word of mouth about their energetic live shows and fiery independent EPs.

In October 2007, they supported Elliott Minor on a tour of the UK but it was not without its problems. Chris Miller became quite ill and though he was advised to miss the band's show at the London Astoria 2 (aka Mean Fiddler) he bravely wanted to soldier on and actually played guitar from the side of the stage, out of view of the audience.

Their hard work seemed to be paying off as the band were beginning to get noticed by some of the UK's most widely read rock magazines. Suitably buoyed by this progress, You Me At Six committed themselves to their first headlining tour of the UK in late 2007 with support from Flood Of Red. They played six shows around the country in venues packed with ever-growing numbers of screaming fans.

Touring was not easy on their personal lives as Franceschi (still aged just seventeen) had left college while Helyer and Miller stayed in education. Fortunately they all had supportive and understanding parents. From the get-go the band had a robust work ethic and they knew breaks from the road were going

Dan Flint
Photo courtesy of Hugh Thompson/Rex Features

to be few and far between. What's the point in being in a band if you're not going to hit the road regularly? They wanted to get their music heard by as many people as possible. Touring was a major factor in their promotional plans and in their aim to better themselves as musicians.

But it wasn't just their parents that You Me At Six needed support from. The band knew from very early on that it was necessary to have the media on their side too; even the small print magazines and obscure websites would prove to be important. To their immense credit, the UK's biggest rock weekly *Kerrang!* got behind the band from a very early stage. After a series of increasingly good reviews and well-attended gigs up and down the UK, plus encouraging sales of their first two EPs, the band were shocked to hear that in late 2007 they had been nominated for 'Best British Newcomer' at the prestigious *Kerrang! Awards*. Things were about to get even more hectic.

TAKE OFF YOUR COLOURS

"Lots of energy and crowd participation! We really feed off a crowd, [we] so love to get them going."
Dan Flint speaking to *The Sound Alarm*

Touring remains the most productive and favourable way of getting a band's music out to the masses. You Me At Six spent a great deal of time on the road in 2008, steadily building up an extensive fan following. "I think because we ... constantly toured, we were the first band from our area that toured abroad," Helyer explained to Simon Rushworth of *Rush On Rock* in 2010. "We've tried to build up a name for ourselves by just touring all the time and people would watch us and enjoy what we were trying to do."

They also learned a few important lessons on tour. Despite the recent *Kerrang!* nomination and growing acclaim on the underground, they were essentially still a relatively unknown band so they wouldn't walk onstage to rapturous applauses from hundreds or thousands of adoring fans but rather audiences with their arms crossed, standing with pints in hands and chatting with their mates while the band perform. They knew that they'd have to give one hundred percent onstage each and every time if they were to capture anyone's attention. It was hard at times not to get disillusioned and frustrated but like any young, up-and-coming band they knew they had to stay positive, confident and focussed. They were shaping up to be a much stronger and unified band.

In fact, they toured so much during this period that defining one tour as different from another would be futile; they were rarely off the road. They toured with The Audition from February 20 until March 4, and both bands became firm friends. Reviews of the band's performances on tour started to appear on the Internet and in printed magazines and it seemed that in a relatively short space of time they were repeatedly being touted as one of the UK's most promising new alternative rock bands.

They hit the Islington Academy on March 4, which was reviewed by Dee Massey at *Caught In The Crossfire*: "Armed with a batch of catchy songs that

> *"The five hundred or so teenagers who have had their tickets for months create a welcome of screams and cheers."*

translate effortlessly well on stage, the band manage to combine British charm with a keen sense of direction. They just can't be faulted for the energy rolling off the stage and sheer presence, and when The Audition's frontman Danny Stevens joins them on stage for a rendition of 'Save It For The Bedroom', the crowds are whipped into a frenzy."

In April, You Me At Six supported Angels & Airwaves during a UK tour; the side-project of none other than Blink-182 mainman Tom DeLonge, Angels & Airways is a successful band in its own right, having released four studio albums between 2006 and 2011 whilst they have also been involved with various multi-media projects. It was their most high profile support slot since supporting Elliot Minor in October 2007. Kudos to You Me At Six for having such highly publicised support slots without a debut album to support, all testament to their increasingly powerful reputation as a robust live band.

On their own headlining tour of intimate venues in the summer, You Me At Six stopped off at King Tut's Wah Wah Hut in Glasgow on June 25, which was reviewed by Emma Jackson at *NoizeMakesEnemies*: "You Me At Six played two new [tracks] off the debut album, due to be released early autumn. It is always a risk playing new material to such a devoted audience, as they may love it or hate it. However, looking around, people were not giving anything away."

They toured with Tonight Is Goodbye in July, which included a stop at Manchester Club Academy. It was reviewed by Joe Lennox for *Designer Magazine*: "The Manchester Club Academy date was You Me @ Six's [sic] first sold out show of their July tour and when the band members appear onstage, the five hundred or so teenagers who have had their tickets for months create a welcome of screams and cheers. The band who must only be one or two years older than their secondary-school-aged audience burst into 'Jealous Minds Think Alike', a song from their forthcoming debut album. It doesn't seem to matter that the song hasn't been heard as much as other songs, the poppy and bouncy opener goes down a treat."

Before the making of their first album they'd already supported the likes of Fightstar, Paramore, Enter Shikari, Saosin, Reel Big Fish, Elliot Minor and The Sleeping amongst others and not only had they become a much better live act themselves but they also learned a few things from some of the more seasoned bands such as how to interact with the crowd and how to compile a focussed set-list.

Despite the burgeoning success, it was perhaps understandable that the band would have some doubts about how long they'd last. "I still don't feel like I am good enough for this position, and on some of the tours I've done it's been a bit overwhelming," Franceschi admitted to Shane Richardson of *Gigwise* in 2007. "But I have no right to complain, so I am not going to!"

This almost constant touring provided an exciting (and exhausting!) backdrop for the recording of the band's first album. Before they commenced working on the debut, the band had recorded the song 'Save It For The Bedroom' at the famed Stakeout Studios in London, where Fightstar, Reuben and Ghost Of A

Thousand had also recorded. They'd played this new track 'Save It For The Bedroom' during live performances but didn't want to record it until they discovered whether their fans liked it or not. However, it got such a rapturous applause that they knew it would be a popular studio song as well as a live favourite. As they were still unsigned, the band funded everything by selling as much merchandise on tour as possible. Despite the rigorous 2008 touring schedule, the band had still found time to lay down some tracks in the studio after the tour as main support to The Audition was completed. They'd actually begun writing tentative songs for their first full-length studio album as early as December 2007 and had about seven or eight songs written when they first entered the studio specifically for that project in early 2008.

Their debut album, *Take Off Your Colours*, was recorded at Outhouse Studios in Reading between March and May of 2008. The band worked with producer and mixer John Mitchell and engineer Matt O'Grady. The latter was in one of the first – if not the very first – UK pop-punk band Fastlane so he was well-versed in the style of music that You Me At Six were making themselves and as such was the perfect man to engineer the band's first album. Tim Turan later mastered the album except for the track 'Always Attract', which was mastered by Richard Dodd. By this point they'd never specifically gone into a rehearsal room and just jammed with an idea.

They'd usually have a song written and laid out before they began rehearsing and recording. In terms of crafting a particular line, it was often the case that Josh would come up with an idea for a lyric and then start penning lines to create a full song. The band would then regroup to practice and see how it evolved from there. They'd get a feel for the lyrics and the style of the song before they began recording. Sometimes they'd even record a few demos to get a deeper feel for the material and perhaps change some parts of the song, with the rest of the band getting heavily involved in the writing too.

Certainly bands like Four Year Strong and All Time Low were an influence on You Me At Six when they were making *Take Off Your Colours*, as well as Blink-182. The band felt they needed to push themselves on their debut album in an attempt to make more complicated and diverse riffs. They wanted to maybe try some new things but also remain faithful to their sound and not deviate from what their growing fanbase had come to expect from them.

The band took the title of their debut album from the cult 1979 Walter Hill directed American film *The Warriors* (itself based on the 1965 novel by Sol Yurick) about gang culture in New York City where gangs would be distinguished from one another by the colours they wear. There is a scene in the film which impacted on Franceschi where a particular gang is told to take off their colours by some kids at an orphanage. By taking off their colours the gang would then lose its identity as a collective force whilst as individuals the gang members would also lose their identity. Franceschi felt that the title *Take Off Your Colours* would stop people from assuming that the band are fake; that they don't have a superficial image. The band felt that they just wanted to be themselves and would expect the same from those around them so the title is not about gangs but rather the concept of personal identity.

Take Off Your Colours opens with 'The Truth Is A Terrible Thing', which has a nifty lead riff that paves the way for the rest of the band to spring into action. The melody is fairly typical of pop-punk music and Franceschi's vocals are slightly nasal but it's a catchy song nonetheless. The riff for 'Gossip' is a definite highlight of the album while the drums are pronounced and the bass plods along, suitably. It's a good track with a memorable melody, while 'Call That A Comeback' is another anthemic pop-punk rocker. 'Jealous Minds Think Alike' has some strong guitars and a bouncing melody while the toe-tapping chorus is perfect for the live stage. 'Save It For The Bedroom' is a robust number with some sturdy vocals and even sturdier guitar work while 'Take Off Your Colours' is a fairly typical but nonetheless enjoyable song. 'You've Made Your Bed (So Sleep In It)' shows the band's skills at making a nifty melody while 'If You Run' is a pedestrian track that is saved by Franceschi's enthusiastic vocals. 'Tigers And Sharks' is a mid-paced ballad with some fiery outbursts of guitars and vocals and 'If I Were In Your Shoes' picks up the pace considerably and has an excellent guitar riff. 'Always Attract' is a slow and heartfelt acoustic number. All the lyrics had been written by Josh and here he also roped in his sister, Elissa Franceschi, to

> *"As long as [the fans] enjoy it I am happy. We don't want to change the world, but to change a few people's day would be really good."*

perform guest vocals. Miller had come up with a riff which Franceschi liked and he'd already penned some lyrics that seemed suited so the song quickly progressed from there. It certainly shows the diversity of the band and how they're willing to channel their energy into other styles of music. A number of songs had been written on the acoustic guitar so the band clearly knew how to make lighter compositions.

Being frank, 'Nasty Habits' is a distinctly average emo-ish tune but the closing track, 'The Rumour', has some interesting guitar work and some pounding drums. It provides an exciting climax to the thirteen track debut album.

Overall, *Take Off Your Colours* shows a promising young band making a collection of strong, assured, perhaps quite Americanised songs. "As long as [the fans] enjoy it I am happy," Josh told *Alt Sounds* at the time of the album's release. "We don't want to change the world, but to change a few people's day would be really good."

You Me At Six's debut album was released on October 8, 2008 via Slam Dunk Records. The band had been signed by the independent label in November 2007; given the band's rising credibility on the road and the success of social media in promoting their two EPs, You Me At Six had inevitability caught the attention of the record industry. The album peaked at Number 25 in the UK album charts which was an amazing achievement; overall it only enjoyed a relatively modest profile though. You Me At Six signed to a new management company in December of 2008 (the legendary Craig Jennings and Carina Berthet of Raw Power Management); the band also secured a US deal with Epitaph (the debut album was subsequently released in the USA on July 21, 2009). The American edition hosts twenty tracks and though it includes all the B-sides it misses 'Kiss And Tell', a track which has become a fan favourite. The band were nonetheless very pleased with the American version.

Reviews of *Take Off Your Colours* were mostly all positive. "They have certainly poured their heart and soul into the album which brims full of enough energy to make recharging your MP3 player somewhat redundant," Jeff Perkins wrote on *BlogCritics*. "There are several immediate attention grabbers on here such as 'Gossip', 'If I Were In Your Shoes', 'Save It For The Bedroom', 'Finders Keepers' and the title track."

In a 7/10 review on the US website *StrangeGlue*, Aidan Williamson was keen to enthuse: "Maybe the Americanised approach was a good idea after all. Since in this country all you have to look forward to is endless swipes from the indie-elitists and tours packed with U16 Girls. Respect is unlikely to be the watchword for You Me At Six, but at least it's better than the gunge tank."

Emma Johnston awarded the album four stars out of five in her enthusiastic albeit short review in the UK daily newspaper, *The Guardian*. She wrote: "Surrey emo kids You Me At Six wear theirs with pride, the bewilderment of tracks such as 'Jealous Minds Think Alike' marking them out as the UK's answer to Fall Out Boy."

Jack Foley wrote an average review of the album for *IndieLondon* and said: "The album is never more comfortable and content than when thrashing about, and the final tracks return to the tried and tested formula – with tracks like 'Nasty Habits' and 'If You Run' benefitting from going for more rockier, gritty elements than the pop sound that guarantees a place on the radio. But while *Take Off Your Colours* does enough to elevate You Me At Six above the average for this kind of sound, it's nothing to get too excited about at this stage."

On July 21, 2009, a two-CD deluxe edition of the album was released in the UK via Virgin, the band's new UK home. The deluxe edition features five bonus tracks: 'Kiss And Tell', 'Finders Keepers', 'Sweet

Feet', 'All Your Fault' and 'Blues Eyes Don't Lie' as well as a remastered version of 'The Rumour'. Unfortunately, the band chose not to include any live tracks on the deluxe edition despite rumours from their on-line fanbase that they might do so.

The band were pleased that *Take Off Your Colours* was re-released in 2009 because of its relatively low-key reception the previous year. Having moved to Virgin, the new label had wanted to make their own mark; Franceschi said to Simon Rushworth of *Rush On Rock* in 2009. "We went to Virgin and they're just so excited about the record that they wanted to do their own job on it. That includes releasing the

"They have certainly poured their heart and soul into the album which brims full of enough energy to make recharging your MP3 player somewhat redundant."

expanded edition and they reckon it can reach a few more people and from our point of view it fills a bit of a gap before the new record's released in 2010."

Several singles were released off the album: 'Save It For The Bedroom', which was the album's first single, charted at Number 145 in the UK. The premise of the song is simple: it is about how couples find out through their behavioural patterns if they are being cheated on. The original 2007 release featured

'You've Made Your Bed' as the B-side while the music video was a compilation of footage filmed by one of the band members from one of their past tours. Fans got to see footage of You Me At Six backstage, hanging out and partying as well as film from their support slots on tours with Angels & Airwaves, New Found Glory and The Audition. The song was later featured on the soundtrack to the video game, *DiRT2*.

'Save It For The Bedroom' was reissued with 'Sweet Feet' as the B-side in March 2009 though the recording differs from the original 2007 single. The 2009 music video is a rather humorous attempt at creating a trashy TV chat show much like the UK's *Jeremy Kyle Show*. Members of the band played angry teenage social misfits and Slipknot fans. The video climaxes with a fight, which is typical of such trashy daytime TV shows.

Other singles taken from the album included 'Jealous Minds Think Alike' which hit Number 100, 'Finders Keepers' which peaked at Number 33 (but reached Number 1 in the *Kerrang!* Top 40 and featured a cover of Fall Out Boy's 'Sugar, We're Goin' Down' as the B-side), while 'Kiss And Tell' reached Number 42 and enjoyed considerable airplay on Radio One. It also topped both the *Kerrang!* and *NME* charts. It's a very teenage-orientated song about a promiscuous, good-looking girl that every guy wants to kiss. The single received a lot of press which was helped by the band's five-date tour of small venues and a few in-store signings. The music video is set at a house party and sees people having fun and partying. Interestingly, the single was backed with a cover of Lady Gaga's 'Poker Face', which was recorded at Radio One's Live Lounge. The band had never recorded a cover version before, favouring only originally written songs instead. (For this first cover version attempt, they were toying with either a Lady Gaga, Katy Perry or Pink song.)

The next singles 'If I Were In Your Shoes' and 'Gossip' failed to chart but received significant airplay. It is the aforementioned 'Jealous Minds Think Alike' (B-side: 'Blues Eyes Don't Lie') that fans felt was one of the album's strongest tracks though it didn't chart especially high on its release as a single. The album eventually spawned seven singles in total, combining the original 2007 edition and later the expanded 2009 edition: 'Save It For The Bedroom' (October 22, 2007), 'If I Were In Your Shoes' (March 26, 2008), 'Gossip' (July 28, 2008), 'Jealous Minds Think Alike' (September 29, 2008), 'Finders Keepers' (May 24, 2009), 'Kiss And Tell' (September 7, 2009) and 'Save It For The Bedroom' (September 14, 2009).

You Me At Six had been labelled a 'pop-punk' band by many critics at this stage in their career. What does that term mean exactly? In the mid-1970s, the original punk was a political and social movement as much as a musical one and though many of the key punk bands were formed in London and New York, other bands sprouted up from around England such as the

Buzzcocks in Bolton. Although many of the punk bands were not filled with virtuoso musicians, much of Britain's youth could relate to the feelings of angst and the danger of the music, consequently persuading future generations of music fans to pick up an instrument and play just for the hell of it. The original punk movement came to an end by the late 1970s (some say as early as winter 1976, after beginning in 1974) but its legacy has grown over the years. Modern punk is very different, with many bands taking influences not only from the original punk movement but other genres too such as the 1980s New Wave or the Seattle grunge scene of the late 1980s and early 1990s. You Me At Six are evidently more inspired by latter-day American punk bands like Green Day, Good Charlotte or The Offspring than English punk band's such as the Sex Pistols or The Clash.

"When we started out the whole pop-punk scene wasn't around and everyone was into metal."

American pop-punk, which had begun with Bad Religion in 1979, is a catchy, anthemic and melodic style of music which appeals to generations of young music fans. From very early on it was obvious that You Me At Six looked across the Atlantic to America for inspiration. "When we started out the whole pop-punk scene wasn't around and everyone was into metal," Max Helyer admitted to Simon Rushworth of

Rush On Rock in 2010. "We wanted to set ourselves apart and write music similar to bands we loved like The Starting Line and New Found Glory. We had a heavier side to us at first but then we found our roots and played the music we wanted to." In summary, whereas the original punk movement was a social, cultural and political movement, pop punk often has less of a social conscience with more emphasis on radio friendly melodic, fast riffs and catchy sing-along choruses.

Which other bands populated this pop-punk genre? Illinois band Fall Out Boy formed in 2001 and released five studio albums between 2003 and 2008, selling over three million copies before announcing a definite hiatus in 2009. The influential *Billboard* newsweekly magazine ranked Fall Out Boy as the 93rd 'Best Artist' of the Noughties. Also often dubbed an 'emo' band, Fall Out Boy are more literate and intelligent than some critics have given them credit for with non-musical influences that include the late cult American author and poet Charles Bukowski.

On the other hand, another prominent pop-punk outfit, Paramore, is a different band altogether with influences ranging from The Cure to their Christian faith (which was proudly important to their music). Fronted by the beautiful and enigmatic Hayley Williams, Paramore released three albums between 2005 and 2009 but perhaps it was the inclusion of the song 'Decode' in the blockbuster teen friendly *Twilight* movie soundtrack that had given them significant mainstream prominence, pushing them to the forefront of the American alternative rock scene.

Pop-punk was a category often thrown at You Me At Six, as indeed was emo, but they refuted both notions. "The term emo is very loosely used nowadays," Franceschi told Scott Williams of *eGigs* in 2008, "I still don't know what it means, it's associated to a certain persona or certain fashion, it used to be about bands that wrote about death and self-harming, so I don't understand how a song like 'Gossip' has anything to do with that."

The band hit the road with Fall Out Boy in late 2008 as the American band's special guests, playing shows in Birmingham, Glasgow and London, which were right in the middle of their own extensive headlining UK trek that had kick-started at the Middlesbrough Empire on October 15 before finishing at the Leeds Met University on November 4.

Fall Out Boy were very friendly with the guys in You Me At Six. "They're massive, they are rock stars and they're the nicest guys," Dan Flint told *Mike Dolbear DRUMS*. "They came up to us, they ran over a few minutes on the soundcheck and Patrick comes up to us and said, 'Sorry for running over, hope it doesn't put you guys out' and we were like 'Whoa! You're Fall Out Boy, you can do what you like.'"

Lewis Bazley positively reviewed You Me At Six's performance at the London Astoria on October 27, 2008 for *In The News*. He enthused: "They launch swiftly into a muscular and biting rendition of 'The Truth Is A Terrible Thing' and the commitment you'd expect from such a young band playing as iconic a venue is evident, while their obvious Idlewild influence shines through on the bridge of 'Jealous Minds Think Alike'."

Playing at the iconic London Astoria continues to be fondly remembered by all members of the band. "We've done bigger venues than that but the Astoria is really special to me, when I was growing up it was the meeting place where everyone from our music scene would go to watch bands," Chris Miller told Megan White at *Counteract Magazine*. "That was a pretty big achievement before it got knocked down."

2008 had been a very good year for the Surrey band given the success of their debut album and the popularity of their live shows. They were also nominated at the *Kerrang!* Awards for 'Best British Band', which was a step-up from their 2007 nomination in the 'Best British Newcomer' category. "*Kerrang!* just seem to have really got behind our band and helped us out quite a lot," Mike Flint told *Mike Dolbear DRUMS*. "It's been really cool. It's insane, we were up against Bullet For My Valentine and all these huge bands like Biffy Clyro and even just to be in the same category as them is just amazing."

Moving in to the New Year, the band toured extensively throughout 2009; they relentlessly trekked the UK with dates beginning at the Bristol

Academy on March 6 and finishing at the London Roundhouse on March 13. Support came from The Spill Canvas and Emarosa.

The band's gig at the Birmingham Academy on March 7 was reviewed by Adam Spall on *Birmingham Live*: "The intro was atmospheric, there was a curtain hiding the band from the crowd. All I could hear was the constant screaming, people screaming for that curtain to fall. It was like a proper show, a full production. As the curtain fell the crowd erupted, You Met At Six looked huge, the light show was fantastic, one thing I noticed was that the band were dressed and acting the same [way they] did last summer on the Academy 2 stage, they looked like the sudden fame hadn't gone to their heads ... just yet!"

This set of dates was dubbed the '777 Tour' with seven shows in seven cities. They were doing things the old school way; they promoted their music and built up a fanbase by spending months on tour, the way bands did back in the 1960s and 1970s. "Lots of energy and crowd participation," Dan Flint told Bekka Collins of *The Sound Alarm* about what fans can expect from a You Me At Six gig. "We really feed off a crowd, so [we] love to get them going."

"The Roundhouse was their most extraordinarily extravagant set to date," wrote Michelle Moore on *Caught In The Crossfire*. "Going all out with their entrance and lights was new for them, but perfectly enabled them to add a little class and a lot more screams to their response. Overall it seems as though

Live shows are the lifeblood of the band
Photo courtesy of Hugh Thompson/Rex Features

You Me At Six have well and truly broken away from just MySpace hot shots and found their ways into the hearts and souls of thousands around the UK."

On March 13, 2009, the band travelled to the United States to perform at the revered SXSW music festival in Austin, Texas. Back in the UK, they performed at the Give It A Name Festival in Sheffield on May 10 and London on May 11. The now-dormant annual festival featured mostly metalcore, hardcore and alternative rock bands and was held in various UK cities as well as other European countries. It was another well-received performance for You Me At Six. Even by this stage of their history the band knew that at headlining gigs of their own they were used to certain luxuries that should not taken for granted.

"There's a big risk element playing festivals," Chris Miller told Megan White at *Counteract Magazine*, "because with a headline show you can turn up and guarantee you're gonna get a soundcheck and check everything's working, whereas with a festival you go on stage, you have half an hour to set everything up and if it works, it works, if it doesn't, it doesn't."

They also took part in the Slam Dunk Festival held on Bank Holiday Sunday on May 24 at Leeds University alongside the likes of Anti-Flag, The Slackers, Sonic BoomSix and Runier. The festival featured six stages of music and was a big step-up from the band's performance the previous year because this time round they were one of the headlining acts. "They opened up two more stages as well so that [was] another thousand tickets [that] could be sold; it was the biggest one in a few years so it's been brilliant," Dan Flint enthused to Mike *Dolbear DRUMS*. "Especially seeing as four years ago Fall Out Boy headlined it, so we headlined it this year, who knows what could happen, if we go in the same direction as Fall Out Boy."

In June, the band played a bunch of sporadic dates around the UK with support acts Not Advised and Me Vs. Hero, including a stop-off at the Manchester Roadhouse on June 10 which was reviewed by Zach Redup at *Deadpress*: "Headliners You Me At Six manage to top it with very little effort. Reeling off well-known singles 'If I Were In Your Shoes', 'Kiss And Tell' and 'Finders Keepers' shows just why You

Me At Six have gotten so far in such a short space of time. Despite their small stage room, the boys manage to [give] their all as much as they would on a stage more than triple its size."

It appeared that good reviews were following the band everywhere and despite a few criticisms that they were merely copying their American pop-punk heroes, You Me At Six were merging out of the shadows of other bands and developing their own sound, no doubt aided by the lengthy road jaunts around the UK and elsewhere.

"There's a big risk element playing festivals ... if it works, it works, if it doesn't, it doesn't."

The band had developed their own interests as they were growing up and knew each other's likes and dislikes on account of how much time they spent together. They also had to learn how to get along with each other, which is often the make-or-break element of band life. There are so many bands that have folded simply because of personal squabbles and conflicts over fairly banal things such as who gets the most attention from fans. Not so You Me At Six. "Josh is always hanging out with everyone when we play festivals and Max is friends with the most amount of people I have seen in my life!" Matt Barnes later told *Street NorthEast*. "I don't understand how, but he knows so many bands its ridiculous. Me and Dan are always the last ones at the bar, always partying. And Chewie (Chris) tends to be the quiet one. He'll sit and play Xbox and chill with a beer."

You Me At Six performed at Download Festival at Castle Donington in mid-June; after that the relentless touring continued, including a slot on the increasingly popular Vans Warped Tour of the USA beginning in Chicago on August 1 and finishing in LA on August 23. You Me At Six performed on the Kevin Says Stage which also featured The Blackout, Jet Lag Gemini and Broadway Calls, amongst many other bands. They managed to sell a few thousands copies of their debut album on the Vans Warped Tour and were really pleased with the reception they were getting in the United States.

"As a group we set ourselves a target of shifting $1,000 worth of merch a day on the Warped Tour and after day one we'd sold $3,2000 worth of T-shirts," Franceschi explained to Simon Rushworth of *Rush On Rock* in 2009. "Some of the other bands wouldn't do that on the whole tour but we were playing to crowds of 600 or 700 people and a lot of them were kids I'd talked to earlier in the day."

It was an exciting opportunity for the band to tour the USA as well as build up some contacts in the industry, meet other bands and make friends and sell their music. Road jaunts like the Vans Warped Tour provide great opportunities for young bands both domestic and foreign to sell their music in America. You Me At Six played to several hundred people at every gig on the Vans Warped Tour. They also got a lot of support from Vans Warped Tour organiser Kevin Lyman who saw the band perform on more than one occasion. It was an intense tour for the band but ultimately the hard work was very productive.

Away from Warped, You Me At Six chose not to head to America and support a big name band on a huge arena tour as most UK bands do over there; instead they played to small audiences to build up a fanbase of their own by playing in as many places as possible all over the country. Yet more hard work.

Back at home they also played on the Festival Republic Stage at the 2008 Reading/Leeds Festival, before they began work on their next studio album; the all important sophomore release. Playing Reading on Saturday August 23 was a huge deal for the band because of its proximity to their home turf in Surrey and the fact it remains one of the UK's most popular festivals. "Yeah, festivals are way different to club shows and venue shows," said frontman Josh Franceschi to Andy Burton at *Virgin.com*. "I think there's more of an atmosphere sometimes, at least more of a crazy atmosphere to it all!"

They drew a big crowd at Reading following on from a band called Black Kids who had managed to pack the tent which caused the band to worry that everyone would leave and not bother to stay and watch You Me At Six. However, their set was rapturously received.

Reading was a busy day for the band and they didn't

get much chance to check out many of the other artists but Franceschi found time to watch Biffy Clyro, Rage Against The Machine, The Blackout, Kids In Glass Houses, Attack! Attack!, All Time Low and The Audition.

On Sunday, August 24, they performed at the Leeds Festival in Bramham Park in the north-east of England where they played 'Jealous Minds Think Alike', 'If I Were In Your Shoes', 'Gossip', 'You've Made Your Bed (So Sleep In It)', 'If You Run', 'Save It For The Bedroom' and 'The Rumour'. They performed in a bigger tent at Leeds with an approximate audience of around four thousand people and the atmosphere was electric. The weekend went incredibly well for the band. They were hyped up as one of the "must see" bands of the weekend and there was a great deal of buzz surrounding their performances at both legs of the proudly iconic English festival.

On September 25, the band hit the road in the United States with The Secret Handshake, The Academy Is..., Set Your Goals and Mayday Parade. This was part of the Alternative Press Fall Ball Tour, which commenced in Pontiac, Michigan at Clutch Cargo's and wound up in Pittsburgh at the Altar Bar on November 15.

They visited some pretty amazing places but one city that made a big impression on them was Chicago where they performed in the House Of Blues. They also had a blast in Portland, Oregon and Orlando,

Florida as well as Virginia where they played at a venue called Norva on Halloween night.

In December, You Me At Six supported their American friends Paramore on a tour of the UK. The band's performance at Cardiff's International Arena was reviewed by Steven Burnett on *The Digital Fix Music*: "The sell-out crowd, comprised mainly of teenage girls, are obviously here for the Hollywood glamour of Paramore but there's still a flurry of excitement for the arrival of the Weybridge upstarts who take full advantage of the gargantuan arena stage and engage in a full-on hyperactive assault."

With this support slot on a major band's headlining arena tour, You Me At Six knew that the audiences were not there to see them but rather the headliners so there was extra pressure on them to perform a tighter, stronger set to gain some new fans. You Me At Six simply did their thing: they performed as they usually do which is as strong as possible. They know how to work a crowd whether the people are specifically there to see them or not. Franceschi is a frontman who knows how to get as much reaction from the crowds as possible.

You Me At Six knew at the beginning that they would never slip into being aloof with their fans that wanted photographs or autographs backstage or anywhere else. Ultimately, it's the fans that make or break a band because they're the ones who buy the music and concert tickets; You Me At Six never forget this. They do as many interviews, meet-and-greets and sign as many photographs as possible. They remain deeply grounded.

The tour with Paramore may have been a success for the band but unsurprisingly they were exhausted from the constant travel and busy, stressful ways of life on the road; they were also a little tired of each other, which was inevitable. They later admitted that at this point they'd actually felt quite divided as a band and knew they needed a break from each other. They wanted to spend time with their own families and have a life away from You Me At Six before they even thought about the release of their new album. If they didn't get some time away from each other then who knows? They may not have regrouped for their second studio album at all. So, wisely, they had some time off at Christmas to prepare themselves for what would no doubt be another non-stop year.

Dan Flint reflected on this period in late 2010 when he spoke to Scott Williams of *eGigs*: "We'd spent months on end living in each other's pockets. So, it was kind of hard for us, and we had to get through that stage of getting all annoyed with each other. We just had to mature about it, and grow up quite quickly. We're all fine now, we're all good, we're better than ever."

It is to their credit that the band were able to step outside of the whirlwind that was their life at this point and recognise the need for time out – the problem for many younger bands is that when success hits, it does so at such a pace that they are rarely able to gain any sense of context or perspective, internal band issues become overblown and the group can implode terminally. With You Me At Six however, they showed a maturity beyond their age and, with the much-needed break thoroughly enjoyed by all, they were ready to hit the ground running again.

HOLD ME DOWN

*"It's just generally really exciting to be able to show
the media that you're not just a one trick pony and you
can actually do something quite interesting."*
Chris Miller speaking to *Counteract Magazine*

You Me At Six's popularity was rising considerably
with interest from major music publications and
a constantly growing fanbase. On November 11,
2009, singer Josh Franceschi announced that their
second full-length studio opus had been completed
and was due for a 2010 release.

Franceschi had been listening to a lot of Envy On
The Coast, Mayday Parade and had even gone and
dug out all his Jimmy Eat World albums to rediscover
that early influence. He was soaking up new
influences and honing his song craft, a fact that would
soon become apparent in the band's new recordings.
When asked by *Alt Sounds* what other band he would
like to be in, given the chance, Franceschi replied:
"Jimmy Eat World, because they are officially the best
band in the world, ever." Jimmy Eat World are
perhaps one of the most revered alternative rock
bands to have emerged from the 1990s alt-rock scene
in the United States. The band formed in Arizona in

1993 and released their self-titled debut album the following year. Six further studio albums followed, with their latest effort being 2010s *Invented*. They continue to have a profound impact on You Me At Six and many of their peers.

Josh was also keen to explain why his band were eager to push on with the new record. "We wanted to strike while the iron was hot," Franceschi told *Hitlab*. "Obviously over the past eighteen months or so we've had some momentum behind us, and we wanted to capitalise on that, to build on it. A lot of bands take two years off [between albums], but what the hell is the use of that?'"

Hold Me Down was recorded at Outhouse Studios in Reading, England with producers Matt O'Grady (also engineer) and John Mitchell (also mixer) from August to November of 2009. There was a great atmosphere in the band's camp and sessions were very productive.

When asked about some of their peers flying to the USA to record, Max Helyer explained to Steve O'Gallagher of *Push To Fire* that, "In the UK we could spend a bit more time in the studio tweaking and finding new ways of doing sound and stuff, and we could get a really good sound out of those guys. We figured it was a formula that worked so why break it? We enjoy recording there and we get along with everyone there, so why not?"

The songs for the new album had been written back in October 2008 and finally finished with a completed set of lyrics in July 2009. The core of the recording took around seven to eight weeks in a solid run whereas it took them only about a fortnight to complete their first album. They had more freedom during the recording of their sophomore album because their schedule was more lenient.

"We spent around eight weeks recording *Hold Me Down* which was probably the craziest eight weeks we have ever spent together as we rented these flats in the town centre near the studio," Dan Flint confessed to Bekka Collins of *The Sound Alarm*. "So most nights after recording we just had parties at our flat, skateboarded inside… We nearly got thrown out so many times."

"A lot of bands take two years off [between albums], but what the hell is the use of that?"

Members of the band had obviously come to know each other rather well since the days of *Take Off Your Colours*. When you share a tour bus or a hotel/B&B room with someone on a regular basis you get to know their most personal habits and thoughts and it's often that kind of intimacy that is reflected in the music. Those thoughts and feelings towards each other helped make the band's second album a somewhat more adult and thought provoking opus as opposed to the typical teenage yearnings of their full-length debut release. *Take Off Your Colours* represented where the band were at, precisely at that point in time. Although their debut album was relatively recent, they were growing up quickly and were more inclined to create their own trademark sound rather than inadvertently mimic that of their pop-punk American heroes.

Franceschi told *Virgin.com*'s Andy Burton: "[This second albums is] more mature just because it really is for us, and my side of things, like we really kind of feel like we developed our sound a lot and we took all the good things, or the things we thought were good, from *Take Off Your Colours* and developed them and developed our ideas."

A major coup came for the band when they hired the renowned studio veteran Bob Ludwig who is famous for working with Metallica, the Rolling Stones, Pearl Jam and Radiohead to master the album. The band wanted to go for a bigger sound; something that was a major step-up from their first record. Having such a revered expert as Bob Ludwig on their side was also them telling their fans that they were outgrowing their youthful pop-punk roots and maturing; Ludwig mastered the twelve-track album at Gateway Mastering.

For this album the band began to show more complex influences, from Incubus, Jimmy Eat World and The Startling Line, which was different from the prevalence of Paramore and All Time Low-type influences manifested on *Take Off Your Colours*. Franceschi had also stopped listening to bands like Senses Fail and The Bled in favour of bands that crafted more melodic-based rock songs but with some heaviness and crunch to the riffs such as Foo Fighters. The songs You Me At Six wrote when they were fifteen and sixteen no longer bore any relevance to the band as they stood in 2009 and 2010.

The second album was also more crafted in terms of preparation. For *Hold Me Down*, they chose to spend more time songwriting than previously; Josh pursued a more introspective route as a consequence of having recently split up with his long-term girlfriend, a creative by-product that fortunately he found to be a very cathartic experience. He chose not to write about his girlfriend explicitly, but rather about how his life had changed within the past year. There were other factors too which became apparent when Josh spoke to *Virgin.com*'s Andy Burton about the album: "I'd say that the main thing that *Hold Me Down* is about like lyrically is, if I'm honest, there was lots of times during the writing process and touring [when] I felt lost, as a person, like I really wasn't really sure if touring round was something that I want to do for much longer."

Some of the lyrics seemed incredibly angry but offered resolution for the singer-songwriter who had gone through these difficult personal times. A year later, he and his girlfriend reconciled, which itself produced some unexpected issues: "When me and my girlfriend got back together," Franceschi reflected to *NME*'s Tom Goodwyn in 2011, "she said to me a couple of times, 'Did you have to write that?', but

Josh
Photo courtesy of Hugh Thompson/Rex Features

I think she understood." He also used his lyrics as an excuse to vent some of his frustration with the music industry, such as on 'Liquid Confidence' and 'Underdog'.

The band hooked up with Aled Phillips of Kids In Glass Houses to perform guest vocals on 'There's No Such Thing As Accidental Infidelity' and Sean Smith from The Blackout to sing on 'The Consequence'.

"Josh pursued a more introspective route, a creative by-product he found to be a very cathartic experience."

How did the making of the album change the band's outlook on life and music? They'd certainly grown up since recording *Take Off Your Colours* and having spent a longer period of time to make their second full-length studio record, they were also honing their talents as well as strengthening their songwriting skills. Franceschi reflected on the band's progress with *Virgin.com*'s Andy Burton: "I think it's definitely a step in the right direction for our band and I think what's good about it is that it still caters for our fans that we have, the people that like You Me At Six now will like *Hold Me Down* and the people that maybe are on the fence about us, or don't like us, we might be able to kinda change their mind as well."

Hold Me Down begins with the feisty lead riff to 'The Consequence', which has a bouncy melody and some heavy drums. 'Underdog' is a bulky song with some catchy lyrics and an indelible chorus while 'Playing The Game' suffers from weaker vocals but benefits from some nifty production effects and orchestrations which add plenty of meat to the song. 'Stay With Me' sounds like a song that fits to the soundtrack of the teen-friendly Superman spin-off TV show *Smallville*; the vocals are certainly heartfelt and there's some good, distinctive guitar work. 'Safer To Hate Her' is an average emo track but it does reaffirm the band's talent at writing catchy choruses. 'Take Your Breath Away' is a speedy rocker with a lot of anger and frustration that comes out of singer Franceschi. 'Liquid Confidence' has a fantastic melody, one of the album's standout tunes and some excellent guitars. 'Hard To Swallow' shows the band going back to the more run-of-the-mill pop-punk sound of the weaker elements of the first album. 'Contagious Chemistry' has some angry outbursts of guitars and vocals which really appeal. 'There's No Such Thing As Accidental Infidelity' is a mid-paced ballad which shows a passionate performance from the band while 'Trophy Eyes' picks up the pace and proves yet again that the band can make some classy pop-punk rockers. Finally, 'Fireworks' is an accomplished way to climax the album; vehement and emotional. *Hold Me Down* shows definite progression from *Take Off Your Colours* with a strong vocal performance, more crafted guitars and decidedly pronounced choruses. A major step forward.

This was the band's first wholly major label record (aside from the repackaged first album), released through Virgin Records on January 11, 2010. It hit Number 5 in the UK charts after strong word of mouth and airplay gave the band further promotion. It hit Number 24 in the Irish album charts too. Silver status in the UK was soon registered, marking 60,000 sales.

Fans had been treated to a free digital download of 'The Consequence' through the band's official website but the first official single off the album was 'Underdog' which reached Number 49, while an acoustic version of the same song was free to stream on the band's website and official MySpace page. It was the band's third most successful single by this point following 'Finders Keepers' (Number 33) and 'Kiss And Tell' (Number 42). It received its first airplay on Nick Grimshaw's BBC Radio One show on December 17 while the music video, which was filmed at Brixton Academy in London in December 2009, was officially released on the band's MySpace page on December 28. The premise behind the video is of a ballerina who is being cheated on by her partner. The ballerina performs a dance routine and then kisses him right in front of the woman he is having an affair with. The video ends after the ballerina has walked away, leaving her presumably ex-boyfriend standing on his own after his "bit on the side" left him.

Two more singles followed: 'Liquid Confidence' peaked at Number 86 and 'Stay With Me' hit Number

52 in the charts. Notably, 'Liquid Confidence' gave the band further exposure when it was added to Radio One's 'A Playlist' in April 2010 and later won the band a *Kerrang!* award for 'Best Single'. It featured B-side live versions of 'The Consequence' and 'Kiss And Tell' both of which were recorded at their gig at London's Wembley Arena (an iconic venue and a testament to the band's hard work that they could film at a venue that had previously hosted gigs by some of the world's most famous artists, including their heroes Blink 182). The music video for 'Liquid Confidence' shows the band recording a video shoot during which they encounter a number of problems which requires them to retake the shot. When it was aired by *Kerrang!* on March 12, 2010 it reached 50,000 hits before April 7. It was also made available on the band's MySpace page. The video for 'Stay With Me' was filmed on location at forest in Chatsworth, California. It performed well in the UK Rock Chart where it peaked at Number 2 behind Linkin Park's 'The Catalyst'.

The band had already begun playing live in support of *Hold Me Down* with a promotional show on January 11; the album's release date. Initially, the band scheduled an in-store performance at Banquet Records but such was the fever surrounding the gig that it was moved to a bigger venue, namely, the Hippodrome in Kingston, London.

Such is the band's interest in modern media and digital technology that they released various bundles via iTunes as well as the *Underdog EP* which consisted of an acoustic version of the single and the nifty new track 'Fact-tastic'. In May, they performed on Radio One's Live Lounge where they recorded a cover of the Ellie Goulding song 'Starry Eyed' which along with an acoustic take on 'Stay With Me' was included as part of an iTunes-released singles collection with 'Stay With Me'.

"The people that maybe are on the fence about us, or don't like us, we might be able to kinda change their mind as well."

Reviews of *Hold Me Down* were mixed. The band's first album was greeted with some undeniably robust reviews – a few lukewarm ones too but mostly positive write-ups – but by now the band had become the darlings of the pop-punk genre and had been featured in a number of popular rock magazines and websites so the stakes were higher. Even the reviews of *Hold Me Down* that were favourable still had some stinging criticisms. Perhaps the Surrey band were part of the wrong generation? Given the rise of the so-called emo culture, You Me At Six have at times struggled to win over some critics because of their largely teenage audience. With a fanbase of primarily thirteen to nineteen-year-olds they were never going to please certain older sections of the media.

Some felt that *Hold Me Down* was too clean-cut in its production and execution and suggested that despite how loud the album sounds, it lacks the kind of rawness that punk rock strives for. As with other pop-punk bands from the UK, You Me At Six were also accused of sounding too Mid-Atlantic. However, in all fairness to the band, some more astute critics noticed the band's progression since the first album and also pointed out that Franceschi's vocals were sounding more mature and adult despite what some called an occasional "whiney" vocal effect. Certainly any band that is dumped in the derided but very popular emo genre of music is going to get a lot of stinging criticisms from certain elements of the music and mainstream press.

There were a fair number of dissenters: "It's too bad that You Me At Six couldn't have come up with a more inventive set of lyrics," wrote Jason Birchmeier on *All Music Guide*. "From a musical standpoint, the songs are as good as last time, especially the first couple, 'The Consequence' and 'Underdog'. Producers Matty O'Grady and John Mitchell are at the helm once again, re-creating the sharp-edged punk-pop sound of *Take Off Your Colours*."

In a review headlined 'The Surrey youngsters fail to establish their own pop-punk identity', Raziq Rauf wrote on *BBC Music*: "Five years ago, this record would have been accused of riding some coat-tails. Today, it's simply a carefully polished and highly competent, nearly retrospective collection of pop-rock songs from a band that, even at a young age, has nothing to say that hasn't been said by others before them (and, inarguably, said better)."

Simon Price said in *The Independent*: "From the action-packed band name to the obligatory long song titles, from the witless blare of the vocals to the compressed blandness of the guitar sound, this is bog-standard emo ordinaire."

"Not even the most fine-meshed musical sieve could unearth any originality here," declared a not exactly enthusiastic Kitty Empire in the *Observer*. "Any of the dozen tracks of *Hold Me Down*, despite being flawlessly executed, could just as easily have been knocked out by teen-adored Hoobastank or Taking Back Sunday," said Joe Barton in *The Skinny*.

Fortunately there were some very positive reviews too: "There are way too many melodic rock/pop-punk bands in the world who are happy to ride on the coat-tails of others; throughout *Hold Me Down*, You Me At Six have instead pushed themselves to create a record that will delight existing fans and should rightfully attract many more," stated Tim Newbound in the teen-friendly magazine, *Rock Sound*. Arwa Haider wrote in the free daily newspaper *Metro*: "Admittedly, their angsty outbursts ('Safer To Hate Her') and cod-American drawling stick to a well-worn formula but it's one spiced up with ample punch, pop and prettiness."

Finally, in a positive 8/10 review on the popular

culture site *In The News*, Ben Brady enthused: "You Me At Six have come a long way in a short time to develop an extremely polished sound, and done well to avoid the trap of resting on a selection of bouncy recycled riffs like so many other young bands, but that work has paid off, with the result being an accomplished record that leaves a lasting impression for all the right reasons." Despite reviews of *Hold Me Down* being notably mixed, it would be churlish to deny that they were showing distinct signs of great potential.

"You Me At Six have instead pushed themselves to create a record that will delight existing fans and should rightfully attract many more."

The band barely had a spare moment to read these mixed reviews anyway: they were just too busy with work. They had started to receive regular airplay on Radio One and consistent exposure in mainstream newspapers. Despite some of the lukewarm reviews, it did seem as though the band were being taken more seriously. Because of their good looks and teenage-based audience they were initially seen as a bit lightweight, but their sustained presence in the album charts rightly helped to gain them increasing amounts of credibility and respect.

The band are more than aware of the fickle nature of

the music industry and how bands often have very little shelf-life. One minute a band can be celebrating a Number 1 album only for them to fail to enter the Top 40 with their second release. It's a cut-throat industry, to use a cliché, but You Me At Six knew that the strength of their material would aid them in their desire for longevity and future chart success. So many bands come and go and the bargain bins of your local supermarket or record store are filled with failures but that is not the kind of future that You Me At Six had in mind for themselves.

"We want to last, and I believe that we will last, and that we have what it takes," Franceschi said to *Hitlab*. "I think listeners will be surprised by *Hold Me Down*. Some of the kinds of preconceptions some people have about what we're really about are wide of the mark, and I'm looking forward to putting that right. How are we going to do that? We're going to do it by working hard: by getting into people's faces and not going away."

While the critics may have had some harsh words to say about the band's second album, by contrast the fans appeared to adore it, hence the high chart position and strong sales. For many, You Me At Six know how to make memorable rock songs for a generation of angst-ridden teens that wanna go to gigs and let loose. The band's songs transferred well to the stage, delivering the kind of punchy, in-the-gut-style performances that gave the tracks added strength and authenticity. Given how the band sways between catchy pop-punk and gritty, angry, alternative rock, it's no surprise that when the band began playing songs from their new album during live performances they were greeted with frenetic screams.

'Underdog' would become a regular fixture in the band's live set-list and a firm fan favourite. The big rock chorus and harmonies of the song proved that the band were capable of making some serious rock tunes. They were eager to play multiple new tracks live because they'd overplayed songs from the first album and wanted to give the fans a chance to become acquainted with the new material.

Things were coming together really well for the band after three to four years of solid hard work. However, although You Me At Six were known to a particular group of music fans, the mainstream audience was largely only just hearing about them.

The band were so busy on tour and promoting their new album that may not even have been aware of the relative lack of attention they had got from mainstream culture but with Virgin Records behind them and a successful second album as well as the reissue of their debut record, they were increasingly gaining wider prominence.

By February, the band had played a selection of in-store events to promote their new release, including a gig organised by HMV to promote British music, which was held at the Relentless Garage in London. The band then scheduled their third headlining UK tour for the start of 2010.

They still hung around with fans backstage before and after a gig knowing that it was important for them not to lose that personal touch with their following. It doesn't matter what the weather is, rain or sunshine, members of You Me At Six can be found chatting with fans outside the venue after a gig. There's always time for the fans. Always.

How do they keep themselves entertained whilst on tour? They have box-set marathons, watching hours of good TV, including the epic American World War II series *Band Of Brothers* produced by Steven Spielberg and Tom Hanks. They also enjoyed watching films with the 2004 critically acclaimed *Crash* being a collective band favourite.

They announced that they would be performing at the Punkspring Festival in Japan and would be supporting Paramore on the Soundwave dates in Australia as well as a headlining Paramore UK tour. It was the first time You Me At Six had travelled to Australia and they could not have been more pleased with the response they were given over there. They were some of the best shows the band had played. To be on the other side of the world and have the chance to play to thousands of fans and get such a zealous response was awe-inspiring. All their hard work was paying off. To experience the beauty and weather of Australia as well as an opportunity to play their music to alternative rock fans Down Under meant that the band were eager to revisit Australia at some point in the not too distant future.

The aforementioned UK tour was actually their biggest headlining tour to date which commenced at the Birmingham O2 Academy on March 9 and finished at London's Brixton Academy on March 20. Franceschi wanted to have the opportunity to play at London's Brixton Academy before he turned twenty-years-old and he managed to do it by the time he was nineteen. What an achievement! The band was in awe of the famous London venue and could not believe it was happening.

As for the band having plans to play a headlining tour of the UK's arenas, they remain confident but not arrogant, as Matt Barnes told Claire White of *Flecking Records*: "Maybe, we'd like to think so but we can't really say 'Yeah, we are gonna do that,' 'cause it might all fail, then we'll look like idiots. We've got our fingers crossed we'll do something like that in the future."

"You want them to leave knowing that they've just watched one of the best You Me At Six performances."

"When kids are coming here expecting a good show you want them to leave knowing that they've just watched one of the best You Me At Six performances," Chris Miller told Simon Rushworth of *Rush On Rock* in 2010. "I met a kid who'd seen us thirty times and she said that Manchester (12/03/2010) was the best show she'd ever seen us play. That's what you want to hear."

They played some decent-sized venues on this tour and well-established gigs too, including Nottingham Rock City, Manchester Apollo and Leeds O2 Academy. These are venues of several thousand capacity each; some of them have lengthy histories of holding legendary rock concerts. The band played to around three thousand fans at the aforementioned Manchester Apollo and had a blast in Glasgow; both working-class cities with hefty rock loving populations. It was a great feeling for the band to be back home in the UK after spending time in America and Australia.

You Me At Six took Forever The Sickest Kids and We The Kings on the road with them as the tour's support acts. "It was a great package tour," Max Helyer enthused to Steve O'Gallagher of *Push To Fire*. "I think from the word go and the first band, the kids were jumping up and down until the end of the night. It was wicked, I wouldn't change it for the world."

However, perhaps the exhausting touring regime was beginning to take its toll. After all, they are only human beings and can suffer from fatigue, jet-lag, sleep deprivation, travel sickness and such. Franceschi contracted laryngitis but defied doctor's orders by going on with the tour, not wanting to let down the fans or slow down the band's momentum. "When I saw the throat specialist," he confessed to Victoria Leggett of *Norwich Evening News*, "they said we shouldn't be going on tour. I'm on some mental antibiotics and a special diet to give me the best possible chance to do stuff."

Reviewing the band's gig at the Newcastle O2 Academy on March 13, George Cannings wrote in *Change The Record*: "What can be said for the band, is that they've got a hell of a lot of confidence and prowess going up on stage – it's something they've always had, even when playing clubs. Frontman Josh Franceschi and guitarist Max Helyer trade onstage banter constantly, and seemingly feel right at home gracing such a large stage. Their performance itself is impressive …"

Tom Walsh was at the same gig but was less impressed, writing in *Rush On Rock*: "The problem with You Me At Six is that you could close your eyes and be at any pop-punk show and not tell the difference. Especially when lead singer Josh Franceschi insisted on replacing his broad London accent with an American twang, a really annoying trait by any English band."

Yet another UK tour was announced for May but this time as in-store signings and intimate performances at various clothes stores around the country; all dates sold out in record time. The tour started on May 9 at the Blue Banana in Birmingham and finished at the Rock Collection in Norwich on May 19. Touring took up most of their life by now but it's good to let loose every now and then. "We go on freshers nights out all the time!" Barnes confessed to *The New Current* in late 2010 about the band's social life outside of music. "Well, not freshers nights out but we go to student nights at clubs, because we basically are students. We're the same age as everyone else."

The band returned to Radio One's Live Lounge on May 18 for the second time to promote their latest album. Presented by Fearne Cotton, the band were interviewed on the show and also performed a handful of songs at the Maida Vale studios in London. They also took part on the Radio One Big Weekend in Bangor, Wales on May 23 where they performed on the 'In New Music We Trust' stage. They were joined onstage by Aled Phillips for a version of 'Save It For The Bedroom' and Sean Smith for 'The Consequence'.

Ask any band and they'll tell you touring is hard work; not just playing the actual performances but everything that goes on before and after a gig such as soundchecks, rehearsals, interviews and all the promotional work as well as the actual travelling; racking up thousands of miles around a single country or even the world. You Me At Six are young guys with an abundance of energy but they still missed being home and hanging out with friends and family and trips to their local pub(s) and such things. However, they're in a band for a reason and they know that there has to be some sacrifices if you are to make it big especially in a famously tough and unforgiving market such as America. Okay, there are times when one member of the band just wants to leave and go home but You Me At Six have always known that they have the potential to become one of the UK's top modern rock acts. It takes a great deal of time and effort to be in a successful band and it provides an opportunity to discover if your friends are true friends because of who you are rather than what you've become. Are they your friends because you're in a big rock band or because the friendship you have together means something? Are friends going to talk to the press about you to make some money or rather defend your name? These are just some of the questions members of You Me At Six must have asked themselves as they were becoming increasingly well known in mainstream music circles.

You Me At Six next took part on the Vans Warped Tour 2010, the annual summer touring festival of music and sports in the USA. "We all love old school Drive Thru bands," Helyer said to Ben Minsky of *Driven Far Off*, "and I remember watching their DVDs from when their bands do Warped Tour and we always wanted to do it, we are very lucky that we have had all these great opportunities in our lives."

You Me At Six played on the Altec Lansing Stage alongside other bands including Parkway Drive, Haste The Day, Whitechapel and We Are In The Crowd. You Me At Six are huge fans of Parkway Drive and both bands had since become friends with each other. Parkway Drive was formed in Byron Bay, New South Wales in 2002 with their debut album *Killing With A Smile* coming out in 2005 via Epitaph Record followed by *Horizons* two years later and

Deep Blue in 2010. They're a melodic group but with a heavy almost metalcore sound and they're an exceptional live band that knows how to work an audience.

"I don't remember where we were, but Warped Tour hired out this massive water park," Franceschi said of his favourite festival memory when speaking to *Bombshell Zine* in 2011. "It was closed, but was right

"I'm on some mental antibiotics and a special diet to give me the best possible chance to do stuff."

next to the festival site. They hired it out from around 9 o'clock at night until around midnight and all the rides were open and that was really cool because we were with all our friends just dishing around and that was really fun."

The band were thrilled to be in the USA; one minute Leatherhead are in their rehearsal room practicing and jamming to some new material and the next minute they're in Salt Lake City performing to several hundred music fans. Touring the USA is an exciting, daunting yet rewarding experience for any British rock band. The extensive touring regime had formed the backbone of the band and was shaping them; making them a stronger unit.

Speaking to Amber Tan of *Purple Revolver* about the band's past experiences in the USA, Flint spoke about how sleeping in bunk beds is a lot different from being in his own comfortable bed back home in England: "It's kinda weird, like being in a coffin. You have to be careful what kind of dream you have when you wake up in a coffin. I often woke up and hit my head on the ceiling wondering, where the hell am I?"

Back home in August, You Me At Six performed at the Reading and Leeds Festivals sharing the stage with the likes of Weezer, Paramore and Blink-182; prior to the Reading Festival they played a low-key warm-up gig at Portsmouth's Wedgewood Rooms. "I enjoyed playing at Leeds more because I get really nervous when my family are there," Dan Flint revealingly told *eGigs*' Scott Williams. "Reading was a great experience but it was almost a relief to have played well in front of our families, but at Leeds I just really enjoyed playing."

On October 31, they held a special Halloween gig at Oxford's Regal. Reviewing the gig for *MusicDune* Hollie Witchalls said: "With You Me At Six barely out of their teens, and already with two successful albums under their belts, it's clear that they have a bright future ahead of them, following closely in the footsteps of the likes of Paramore, it won't be long until they'll be playing their own sold-out arena tours."

The band commenced a full tour of the UK in December, which was their last tour in support of *Hold Me Down*. They were feeling the need to make some new music but still had more shows to perform.

However, transport logistics for the tour were troubled by the effects of severe weather conditions in Scotland: they were forced to reschedule the two shows at the Edinburgh Corn Exchange.

Aside from the weather trouble in Scotland, the band were ecstatic about the reaction they'd been getting from British audiences. Fans treated them with open arms all over the country from the provincial towns to the metropolitan cities. During the first of the two rescheduled gigs in Edinburgh, the band announced that they would be playing at the 2011 T In The Park Festival. Josh Franceschi spoke to the *New*

"I often woke up and hit my head on the ceiling wondering where the hell am I?"

Scotsman about the band's growing success in Scotland: "We have always done well in Scotland. Even when we were booking our own tours three years ago, we played Glasgow Barfly and it sold out. That was the first time we were in Scotland and we weren't expecting it."

Other dates on the hugely successful UK tour included Wolverhampton Civic Hall, Bournemouth BIC, Doncaster Dome, Manchester Apollo and London Hammersmith Apollo. Support came from Canterbury, Set Your Goals and The Blackout. You Me At Six were slightly better known in the UK than

The Blackout but the case was different in Europe were The Blackout where better known in certain countries. All the bands aimed to help each other out.

"They're just good fun dudes to be with, they know how to have fun," Max Helyer told *Alternative Music Hub* about touring with Set Your Goals. "They know how to keep it real as well and kicking back with the lads and having a good time. I mean you go out and you go walking around the place or just kicking back in the venue just having a good laugh and having a joke about with them was always good."

Festival tours are great and the band have had a lot of fun in the past but with their own headlining tours You Me At Six know how many people are going to be in the audience, how many tickets have been sold, they even recognise some of the fans and they get soundchecks and time to rehearse. They have more control. With festivals, most bands don't really know what is going to happen and don't often get soundchecks. Bands don't really know who's going to watch them or what the sound and venue acoustics are going to be like. You Me At Six have played in a diverse variety of environments and have learned how to handle all situations and as long as they're having fun and the audience are digging the music than it's mission accomplished.

"About halfway through the set, YMAS put down their electric guitars and instead reached for the acoustic ones," wrote Gena Hollyoake enthusiastically on *New Beats Media,* about the band's gig at the iconic

Wolverhampton Civic Hall on December 7. "At this point everyone knew something special was going to happen. The band performed acoustic versions of 'You've Made Your Bed (So Sleep In It)' and 'Always Attract' with both songs leaving the audience speechless in fear that they may miss a single word."

"I think they are big songs," Dan Flint said to Claire White of *Flecking Records* about using these songs in the live set-list. "You've only got to look on YouTube to see how many plays they get compared to some of the other songs from the album, so we just think the kids like them."

The band's gig at the enormous Manchester Apollo on December 13 was reviewed by Naomi Havergal on the on-line lifestyle magazine *Female First*: "You Me At Six's opening was flawless, beginning their set with 'Save It For The Bedroom' which caused a crowd surge, tidal waving to the stage. It wouldn't have surprised me if a few injuries occurred, but anything is worth a close-up. However, it wasn't all constant jumping, punching and girls pulling hair; towards the end of the set the band toned it down with an acoustic set."

Reviewing You Me At Six at the Hammersmith Apollo on December 22, Hollie Witchalls wrote on *MusicDune*: "The final *Hold Me Down* tour has proven to be You Me At Six's best tour so far, with a perfect set-list and extraordinary lighting, that even the band themselves said was a main component. Confetti is released as the song draws to an end…"

Matt Barnes joked about the female attention the band get at shows when asked by *The New Current* (December 2010) if they ever get underwear thrown at them during gigs: "Well, we do but Dan doesn't see them because he's at the back and they can't throw that far. No, there's not that much female attention. It depends. If we were to go out to a rock bar after the show then there are people who know who we are. So we tend to go to dance clubs and dance like idiots."

Aside from the heavy touring that the band committed themselves to throughout 2010, they did find the time to hit the studio again but this time for a one-off project. A surprise collaboration came at the tail-end of 2010 when they teamed up with Chiddy from the American rap duo Chiddy Bang for a song called 'Rescue Me'. Initially it was reported that the band was perhaps reluctant to use the collaboration as a single. They wanted to finish the run of singles from *Hold Me Down* with 'Fireworks' which is a ballad that they felt was the right way to end the promotional run. Their record label had other preferences and wanted a stronger, heavier rock song that they thought would make a bigger dent in the charts.

The band spent two days working with Matthew Lawrence at a studio in North London before they sent the track to Chiddy for him to record his vocals. The band had not worked this way before. It was an experience for them which made a lasting impression.

However, Josh told Danni Murphy of *The White Haven Guide*: "We're sitting around really bored, as we were waiting to go on tour and our label asked us if we wanted to just go mess around in the studio with this guy that is in town at the moment. We were like 'Yeah!' We went down and we wrote a song with our producer, our label really liked it and they got us a rapper from our label, a guy called Chiddy and it just went from there…"

Artists rarely know how diverse collaborations such as 'Rescue Me' are going to be received by their fans. It can either be a hit or miss situation, really. Although certainly very successful, Chiddy was not yet a mainstream rapper on a par with the likes of 50 Cent. It was an experiment; a one-off single. Many well-established artists have also tried leftfield collaborations such as this one in the past and many will continue to do so; Queen have done some seemingly oddball things in their career pre- and post-Freddie Mercury's death. Led Zeppelin's Jimmy Page gave permission for Puffy Daddy to use the riff from the Led Zeppelin song 'Kashmir' for his track 'Come With Me' and the remaining members of Queen allowed Wyclef Jean to remix 'Another One Bites The Dust'. The New Jersey band 30 Seconds To Mars worked with rapper Kanye West on 'Hurricane'. Some rock fans hate the very notion of their favourite bands hooking up with rappers but the fact remains that rap music is exceptionally popular, and besides, why limit collaborations to genre definitions? If it means that such collaborations bring both genres of music to a wider audience then where is the problem?

Although You Me At Six confirmed that the Chiddy collaboration would not be appearing on their third album, it was finally released on February 14, 2011 and hit Number 21 in the UK charts, thus making it their highest charting single to date and their first Top 40 hit since 'Finders Keepers'. It sold close to 20,000 copies during its first week of release in the UK. 'Rescue Me' also reached Number 50 in the Irish singles chart. The B-side track 'Knew It Was You' was a song written during sessions for their second album while the other B-side is an instrumental version of 'Rescue Me'. The single was included on Chiddy Bang's debut album *Breakfast*, released in 2012. It was the rap duo's second UK Top 40 hit following on from 'Opposite Of Adults' which hit Number 12 in May 2010. The music video, which was first aired on YouTube on January 20, 2010 and which does not feature the band or Chiddy, is about a black boxer preparing with his coach for his upcoming fight and ends when the boxer is in the ring and the bell sounds.

Fans greeted the new single with mixed feelings given that it didn't sound like previous You Me At Six work. Inevitably unexpected collaborations between such diametrically opposed artists work for some people and not for others. It is the nature of the beast.

"I think when we did 'Rescue Me', it left people not knowing what to expect next," Franceschi told *Digital Spy*. "It was such a wild card song and it was like nothing we'd ever done before and nothing we'll ever do again." The band do not now play the song live.

You Me At Six don't just listen to rock music; members of the band also enjoy rap, hip-hop, reggae and pop. What 'Rescue Me' did was to show that the band were willing to broaden their creativity and evolve as musicians regardless of any criticisms they might face for their endeavours.

"It was such a wild card song and it was like nothing we'd ever done before and nothing we'll ever do again."

2010 had been a very exciting year for You Me At Six; they'd now achieved many positive milestones and with 'Rescue Me', they'd already proved that they were not afraid of keeping the momentum going, or the instinct for experimentation alive.

Had the band's rising profile wrecked havoc on their social life back in Surrey? "I'll go running for six or seven kilometres and just feel the endorphins," Franceschi told Ben Brady of *In The News* in 2010. "I have a girlfriend so I'll see her and my friends, we go to the cinema, bowling, just everything a standard nineteen-year-old would do. I basically live the life of a nineteen-year-old at uni."

They'd come such along way since the (relatively recent) days of *Take Off Your Colours*. "As a band we want to make everything we do the right way, we achieved tons of things we never thought as a band we would do," said Max Helyer to Danni Davies at *Resonance UK* about the band's triumphant 2010. "When we come back again with our new album, we have lots of things planned for it, hopefully they will be as exciting as 2010 was for us!"

SINNERS NEVER SLEEP

"We're really happy with what we've produced. I would say this [third album] *is the most honest record we've made."*
Max Helyer speaking to *Digital Spy*

You Me At Six had always cherished their strong profile as a blistering live act and 2011 proved to be no exception to the rigorous touring schedule which they had committed themselves to throughout the previous year. They toured the UK at the start of 2011 and made their first trip to Cardiff Great Hall since supporting Paramore back in December 2009. The band were supported by Not Advised and Canterbury. A staff writer for *Entertainment Cardiff* enthused: "Screams in the crowd and a blacked-out arena; You Me At Six open with 'Save It For The Bedroom' which gets the crowd on their feet and all singing together. I like to think that You Me At Six chose this song to open with as this is the song that really started their career. You Me At Six have a set that is so tight and shows how far this band have come with every song being a huge sing-along with the crowd."

Reviewing the band's energetic gig at the iconic Hammersmith Apollo, Chloe Chaplin wrote on *With*

Drums And Colour: "Ending on 'Underdog', where they had a confetti cannon go off, you were stood there wishing you could watch the whole set again. The amount of energy the members put in to each song was incredible, as were the lights they had."

Back in February the band announced that they were to tour with Parkway Drive, Bleeding Through and Confession as part of the famed Parkway Drive-organised 'The Mix 'N' Mash Tour' of Australia which went ahead in May. However, both You Me At Six and Bleeding Through withdrew from the tour because of their extended recording schedules.

Also, a planned extensive arena tour of the UK in the summer as support for Blink-182 was cancelled and rescheduled for 2012 with an extra date in Glasgow after Blink announced they were going to complete work on their latest studio album. A segment of the American band's press statement read: "When we booked the tour last year, we were confident that we would have the new album out before the summer. Turns out we were mistaken as the album is taking longer than we thought and won't be out till later this year."

You Me At Six were very pleased to be offered the Blink-182 tour which they didn't specifically need to do as they'd already had some festival appearances lined up and their own headlining UK shows, plus they were working on their third album. However, they were evidently psyched that they'd been offered the chance to do a major UK arena tour with their heroes.

Dan Flint had met Blink-182's Travis Barker at Reading Festival and so when he found out they were going to hit the road with one of his heroes he was ecstatic, but sadly he'd have to wait a while longer. Flint told *eGigs*' Scott Williams about his experience at Reading in 2010: "I met Travis Barker during the day, I got invited up on stage to watch him play. I had a massive fan moment, and I was freakin' out like a little kid, I was sitting about two foot behind him whilst he was playing. That was a very surreal experience." The subsequent cancellation was a frustrating time for You Me At Six although it gave them time to work on their own material for their upcoming third album.

The band originally assumed that the tour was just going to be put on hold for a few months but they were told by their management that Blink-182 were not going to be able tour the UK until at least twelve months ahead. The problem was that You Me At Six were already booked well in advance and were simply too busy with recording their own album to commit to the rescheduled dates, so sadly they had to pass. "Obviously, you know, in a year's time you tend to have other plans," Matt Barnes told *Street NorthEast* in 2011. "We couldn't put twelve months on hold for Blink-182, so we were all absolutely devastated and really upset."

"Basically we didn't do nearly as many festivals as we would have in Europe this summer," Franceschi admitted to *Bomshell Zine* in July 2011, "and nobody wanted to book us because we were doing the Blink-182 tour. Then when they cancelled, we tried to jump on as many festivals as we could, and we managed to jump on a few, but it's a shame and we get it that they had to finish their record and that's what's most important for them…"

Despite working on their own new album, You Me At Six continued to play more live shows with a focus on a number of high-profile festivals. On June 15, they performed to 250 fans at The Kingston peel which was dubbed 'Sonisphere Secret Session'. In no particular order, they played such fan favourites as 'Save It For The Bedroom', 'Finders Keepers', 'Stay With Me', 'If I Were In Your Shoes', 'Fireworks', 'Liquid Confidence' and 'Underdog'.

They performed at the Sonisphere Festival in the UK before the release of their upcoming third studio album. The event was staged between July 8 and July 10 at Knebworth Park with headliners Metallica (Friday), Biffy Clyro (Saturday) and Slipknot (Sunday). You Me At Six performed on the Saturday on the Apollo Stage which also featured Sylosis, Architects, Cavalera Conspiracy, Bad Religion, Weezer and Biffy Clyro performing their first major festival headlining gig. You Me At Six were slotted between the latter two bands.

Matt Barnes spoke to *Rock Kent* about the band's experience playing Sonisphere: "Definitely living the dream! Sonisphere was a lot different for us because it's more metal than other festivals we've played, with bands like Metallica and Megadeth. We played on the more poppy day with Sum 41 and luckily no one with a Megadeth T-shirt threw beer at us!!!"

Lais MW reviewed You Me At Six's performance for *Bring The Noise*: "The crowd love them and umbrellas are discarded for their catchiest of catchy hits 'Kiss And Tell', 'Save It For The Bedroom', 'Hard To Swallow' and the rest. Armed with some

> *"Definitely living the dream! ...*
> *Luckily no one with a Megadeth*
> *T-shirt threw beer at us!"*

stellar songs they even manage a circle pit at one point, which is saying quite a lot considering the fact that they're playing a festival mainly populated by people who have come to see Metallica or Slipknot."

On Sunday July 10, You Me At Six performed on the *NME* Stage at T In The Park in Balado, Scotland. Inevitably, they attracted a different type of music-loving crowd than what was on offer at Sonisphere and other festivals they'd appeared at in the past. It's the diversity of a festival like T In The Park which makes it a challenge for a band such as You Me At Six.

On August 15, the band ventured to Belfast to perform at The Belsonic Festival, an open-air event that takes place in the city centre. It was reviewed by Mark Ashby for *Hevypetal*: "English pop-punks You

Me At Six had the unenviable task of opening ... and they didn't quite rise to the challenge. While the front dozen rows went absolutely berserk as soon as they hit the stage, frontman Josh Franceschi's non-stop bouncing failed to inspire no more than an apathetic performance from his four normally high energy band mates."

The band journeyed to Poland to perform at the excellent Coke Live Music Festival in Krakow on August 19 where they performed the tracks 'The Consequence', 'If I Were In Your Shoes', 'Save It For The Bedroom', 'Safer To Hate Her', 'Kiss And Tell', 'Liquid Confidence', 'Trophy Eyes', 'Loverboy', 'Stay With Me' and 'Underdog'.

"Yeah, we have been blown away by it," Dan Flint said to Gena Hollyoake of *News Beat Media* about the band's festival tour of Europe in 2011. "We have done some Euro festivals in the past and a few people came to watch us but didn't really know what was going on. This year we have been filling tents with crowds that know the words and they go nuts, which makes it a lot of fun."

They also performed at the famed V Festival in Hylands Park, Chelmsford which was staged between August 19 and August 22. Other bands on the bill included Pendulum, Manic Street Preachers, Big Audio Dynamite and Imelda May. V Festival is a pop fest whereas Sonisphere is for metalheads and You Me At Six occupy territory somewhere in the middle. How many bands can play at a festival with Slipknot and Metallica one day and then play on the same bill at another festival with Jessie J and Bruno Mars?

"'This is a fucking pop festival,' hollers You Me At Six frontman Josh Franceschi during his act's Saturday afternoon V Festival set, 'and look how many people are watching a rock band!'" wrote Chris Salmon in *The Guardian*. "He means it in a good way – Franceschi is clearly relishing the energetic response from the crowd. But, in truth, the band's second stage audience is dwarfed by that of boyband The Wanted, currently playing in the gargantuan Arena tent."

The biggest event of 2011, however, was not the band's tour schedule but the release of their third album. Although *Hold Me Down* did not receive overwhelmingly positive reviews, the band had an increasingly large and dedicated fanbase that wanted to hear something special from them. Where could they go from there? They were not kids back at high school anymore and if they were to be taken seriously and make a mark in the mainstream consciousness then they had to deliver something a little different from *Take Off Your Colours* and *Hold Me Down*. The band knew this and as such they were already preparing ideas for a big step in a new direction.

Publicity for a third album by You Me At Six had already began to worm its way through the Internet by late 2010 when singer Josh Franceschi confirmed that they had already begun writing and recording some demos which would gave the band a heavier sound.

By early 2011, stories began to circulate that the band were going to collaborate with a number of artists on their third full-length studio album. Moving into August, they had about twelve songs written and ready for recording.

"There's not really a theme to it," an open Dan Flint told Scott Williams of *eGigs* in December 2010. "I think it's a bit more of a progression continuing from *Take Off Your Colours* to *Hold Me Down*. From *Hold Me Down* to the next one is going to be slightly different, because we're that much older again."

"They were good friends of ours and the songs they did suited their style of voice and what they could bring to that song."

Names like Oli Sykes from Bring Me The Horizon and even Adele were thrown around but the one potential collaboration that caught fans' attention was with Paramore's Hayley Williams. Franceschi had spoken about his desire to duet with her after the band had played at the Reading and Leeds Festival. It wasn't until April 8, 2011 that the band revealed that Oli Sykes – whose band was on a tour of the States with A Day To Remember – was recording with them at the Sound Factory in Los Angeles where they were working on their third album. Sykes is a good friend of the band. In fact, You Me At Six tend to hang around with metal and hardcore bands more than punk bands. Members of You Me At Six would crash at Sykes's house in the old days and Josh Franceschi had collaborated on a Bring Me The Horizon song in the past so now Sykes offered to return the favour.

As well as the Oli Sykes collaboration, the band hooked up with Winston McCall from Parkway Drive for a track called 'Time Is Money', which they actually contemplated not including on the finished album because of its heaviness. It's the most brutal song they have recorded from any of the material on their first three albums.

However, it didn't mean the band were going to be a heavy rock band from thereafter. You Me At Six will probably never be a heavy rock band. It's not in their collective genes.

They sent the song to McCall after Franceschi had written the melody. On the last Vans Warped Tour the music that members of You Me At Six were listening to was mostly Parkway Drive and The Ghost Inside The Van, which would heavily influence them.

"Winston [McCall of Parkway Drive] and Oli were on the record because they were good friends of ours and the songs they did suited their style of voice and what they could bring to that song," Max Helyer told *Air3 Radio*. "If there were ideal people to collab [sic] with I would love to do something with either Jay-Z or John Legend."

'Time Is Money' is a song that is reflective of where the band were at in 2011. They'd come a long way since *Hold Me Down* and they made references to it in the lyrics. The music industry, record label and public were dealing with a different band since the days of *Take Off Your Colours*.

They have never resented the music that they'd made in the past but at the same time they had moved on from it and had developed into a different band altogether. Lyrics tend to be shaped by real life experiences and evidently You Me At Six had grown up since the teenage years of *Take Off Your Colours*, so inevitably the lyrics on their third album would be more reflective of their twenty-something lifestyles. As already noted, writing lyrics can also be a therapeutic experience for a wordsmith and maybe on their new album Franceschi would have other subjects to sing about?

After touring so much for the first two albums, the band were excited about the new material and given their shared life experiences on the road and in the studio they had found new inspirations and wanted to channel those ideas into the lyrics for their third full-length album. Being in a band is partly about being creative and sharing your inspirations with others which may in turn affect their lives. How many people have changed the course of their life because of a song by The Beatles or a particular lyric by Bob Dylan? How many youngsters have picked up a guitar because they saw some footage of Hendrix on TV or YouTube? Musicians can affect people in so many different ways.

Writing new ideas up had taken place from around September/October of 2010 to February/March of 2011. "There were points where we were writing songs and we didn't know if we were going to have enough songs in time," Max Helyer told *Alternative Music Hub*. "We were kind of worried, we wrote like sixteen songs before we went in and we were like 'Have we got enough songs?' and 'Are these the best songs we can write as a band?' and at some points when we got in the studio to record the new songs we were changing parts of songs that we weren't happy with and changing little bits to make sure these songs can be the best they could be."

"After touring so much for the first two albums, the band were excited about the new material and given their shared life experiences on the road and in the studio they had found new inspirations."

The band knew that they did not want to write about the themes that had dominated much of the first two albums as well as the typical ways of teenage life like going to parties and chasing girls. Actually at this point in time, Josh Franceschi wanted to hit the road and play some shows but the rest of the band preferred to work on the new album so being a democratic unit they decided to record the album first and then go on tour. They knew that if they didn't record the album as soon as possible they would not have time to do so because of the heavy touring that was organised for the following months ahead.

Franceschi will generally write the lyrics while the rest of the members write their own actual parts and then the songs will fall into place (the songwriting credits in the sleeve notes for *Sinners Never Sleep* state 'Music by You Me At Six. Lyrics by Josh Franceschi'). Ultimately they created the songs together.

> *"I really enjoyed working with Garth ... he's so passionate. When someone comes in with that much experience you have to listen to them."*

Sinners Never Sleep was recorded at the Sound Factory in Los Angeles, California with Garth "GGGarth" Richardson from March to May of 2011. It was definitely the longest time they had spent in a studio working on an album. It was a very hectic period for the band but they'd learned an awful lot about making music. "We were looking for a few producers and while we were playing a show at Hammersmith Apollo, he turned up to one of the shows," Matt Barnes told *Street NorthEast* about hooking up with Richardson. "He introduced himself and said he was in the running for working with us on our next album, so he wanted to come down to see us."

Richardson is best known for his work with Rage Against The Machine, Red Hot Chilli Peppers and Biffy Clyro. As a band You Me At Six were always willing to explore new avenues and try different things and after having recorded two albums in the UK they wanted to try elsewhere – the USA seemed like the perfect place.

"I really enjoyed working with Garth," Dan Flint (who recorded his drums in the old-school way on analogue tape) enthused to *Soundsphere Mag*'s Dan Shields. "He's so passionate. When someone comes in with that much experience you have to listen to them."

Richardson took the band out of their comfort zone and taught them a few new tricks in the studio. A talent with a positive "can-do" attitude, Richardson forced the band to pour their hearts and souls in to the new album. They liked the honesty in each other and Richardson knew the band could pull it off onstage as well as in the studio. Both producer and band have an undiluted passion for music. The band put a lot of thought into how they should portray themselves on this latest collection of songs and they were adamant that they wanted a tough rock sound. They wanted some big melodies, strong hooks and bouncy choruses. The band wanted an honest rock album but not so different from their previous material that they'd scare away their fans. They felt it was a natural progression from the band's sound since *Hold Me Down* and even back when they made their second album they knew that the follow-up would be a more rock-orientated effort. What Franceschi loved about Jimmy Eat World, for example, was how they'd progressed from their third album 1999s *Clarity* to 2007s *Chase This Light* but not lost what they were about as a band. They'd grown into themselves as time progressed and gotten older.

The Sound Factory is full of rock 'n' roll history and You Me At Six were stoked to be recording in LA. "We got these really great apartments with a super nice gym, a pool, a hot tub, it was so nice," Franceschi enthused to Tom Goodwyn at *NME*. "We went out and bought an Xbox, watched loads of football, had poker nights and we got really into it." As noted, working in Hollywood was a lot of fun for the band but it didn't have a fundamental influence on their music as such. Richardson had a direct impact on the band's new material. "It's a really exciting point because it did develop my guitar skills and my sounds…" Helyer admitted to *Straight Up Random*. "But then for Josh as well, he had Matt O'Grady, used on the last two CDs, doing his vocals and that's who he feels comfortable with. So he was in his zone, we were getting in our zone and combined the two together; Garth pushed us to the limit." Helyer alone spent about three weeks laying down his guitar parts.

As Helyer points out, the band took Matt O'Grady with them to the States and they also had John Mitchell to mix the album with O'Grady so the band had not lost all of the connections to their earlier sound. Meanwhile, Ben Kaplan was credited with recording the twelve-track opus (actual sleeve notes state: 'Produced by GGGarth, mixed by John Mitchell and Matt O'Grady and recorded by Ben Kaplan.').

Helyer had a few riffs that he'd kept for years but could never find the right songs for. However, he managed to use one riff for 'This Is The First Thing' on *Sinners Never Sleep* that had been taken from the vaults and dusted off. Guitarists often archive riffs for future use (Some riffs never actually leave the vaults and are kept unreleased).

Richardson didn't attempt to change the band's sound but rather to advise them and offer them ideas to develop and refine the You Me At Six musical identity. The band learned to play around with their sound and do things that hadn't been done in the past. They wanted their music to still sound like You Me At Six but also an older sounding version; one that didn't sound like teenagers playing music in their parents' garage. As musicians they wanted to push themselves to the limit to create better music.

They'd never worked with Richardson before so it was good to have someone outside of the band's camp come in with new ideas; a fresh and creative working approach which the band enjoyed. Also being out in LA, thousands of miles away from their home town, meant they had few distractions and could concentrate on making the new material.

They created a strong set of songs and spent a lot of time on each track, wanting each individual song to sound as good as possible; making sure they'd reached their full potential. As a band they certainly felt they'd never sounded so good. What they created in the studio was what they believed was their best work to date.

Recording in America was also a great experience for the band because a lot of British bands had recorded on the other side of the Atlantic in the past such as Queen and Led Zeppelin. "We've always been really relaxed about it once we've got in the studio and just jammed and before you know it all the songs have just come out," Chris Miller admitted to Megan White of *Counteract Magazine* about the band's approach to writing new material. "We find it quite easy whereas some people find it quite tough."

It became obvious at this point that You Me At Six were striving for a heavier, hard-hitting rock sound. They'd grown up a lot since the days of *Take Off Your Colours*. They started out as a pop-punk band but with *Sinners Never Sleep* they wanted to go for a more mainline rock sound influenced by the Foo Fighters or maybe even Kings Of Leon.

As well as the aforementioned and exciting Oli Sykes collaboration, the band also teamed up with Reece Carter on 'This Is The First Thing', Dean Dobbs on 'No One Does It Better', Jack Howard on

'When We Were Younger' and Parkway Drive's Winston McCall on 'Time Is Money'. The band cooked up a total of nineteen songs in the studio though they chose to include twelve on the finished album. Regardless, on 'No One Does It Better', Helyer enthused to *I Like Music*: "It's still got that significant You Me At Six sound but it shows those other directions that we can go in as a band, what we can produce and write ourselves, you know?"

> *"We find [writing new material] quite easy whereas some people find it quite tough."*

However, the album did not go without hiccups as Franceschi became ill during their stay in Hollywood and he was ready to come home. "In our third week out there, I got really ill," he admitted to *NME*'s Tom Goodwyn. "I had loads of chest problems and on the day of the Royal Wedding I was actually in hospital having treatment. I think me being ill cost us about twelve days in the studio and meant I had to do all my vocals in about two or three weeks."

There was no time to lay low; the band didn't want to spend too much time off work losing momentum. Besides, they didn't really have much of a choice, given their schedule. "We thought we would have had a bit of time off because we've been recording for five months," Franceschi told *Bombshell Zine* in July, "but it seems like we're going to shoot some videos, and [be] doing lots of these press days on the phone, which is absolutely fine because there's nothing better than talking about your band and promoting what's coming up, so we've been keeping busy gearing everything up…"

Publicity was further heightened in August when 'This Is The First Thing' was leaked on-line while the band were still recording the album in LA and then in September 'Bite My Tongue' was also leaked on-line. During an age of digital downloads and a lack of control on the Internet, it is not uncommon for music to be leaked; the ironic fact is that it can sometimes offer inadvertent free publicity on behalf of the artists involved but the downside is that artists also struggle to gain back control of their music after it has seeped on to the web.

So, how did the band come up with the title for the new album? Initially, they were going to call it 'Little Death', which has sexual connotations in French that the band found humorous. They spoke with other insiders close to the band who said it made them think about their daughter being abducted, so naturally the band didn't want their album title to make people think about such horrid events.

However, there is a more personal side to 'Little Death' which is a song on the album. There are lines in the song that were written in response to the passing of both Flint and Miller's fathers. "It has nothing to do with religion," Franceschi said to *The*

Independent's Ed Cooper, "a good man [Mr. Flint] passed away for no reason. I hate people trying to make a reason for it. I like to think they're watching over us and looking after our fortune and bringing us good luck when we need it." They threw some other titles around and eventually came up with *Sinners Never Sleep*.

The band's third album opens with 'Loverboy' which has some of their best guitar work to date. 'Jaws On The Floor' has some cool production effects and a catchy melody while 'Bite My Tongue' is an angry rocker with a lot of screaming vocals.

'This Is The First Thing' slows down the pace somewhat but it shows another side to Franceschi's maturing voice. 'No One Does It Better' is a heartfelt song about love while 'Little Death' sees the band going back into angry mode. 'Crash' is another ballad that continues to show the band's thirst for travelling outside of their pop-punk comfort zone. 'Reckless' is a strong radio-friendly rocker and 'Time Is Money' opens up with a gritty riff and some manic drums. 'Little Bit Of Truth' is a slow love song while 'The Dilemma' is a return to the emo sound of the first album. The final track, 'When We Were Younger', is a notably sombre way to end an adventurous album.

Sinners Never Sleep is a darker album than the band's first two releases; angrier too. The band were certainly showing an aptitude at recreating their sound with each new release. *Sinners Never Sleep* does significantly differ from *Take Off Your Colours* though there are moments where the band slips back into old territory. Overall, it is easily the band's best album to date and shows great promise for future releases.

A song like 'Bite My Tongue' would appeal to fans of hard rock, while a more mid-paced, melodic rock like 'Crash' and 'Nobody Does It Better' would certainly allure fans of Snow Patrol or Coldplay to their camp. Their first love was pop-punk but things are different now in the band's camp as Franceschi admitted to Shane Richardson of *Alternative Press*: "We're trying different things, trying to move forward. It's not that we don't be part of [pop punk], I just don't think we belong with the UK's pop-punk scene."

Perhaps the band were hoping that a song like 'Bite My Tongue' would get hardcore metal fans into You Me At Six. Maybe those fans would enjoy the rest of *Sinners Never Sleep* despite the style of music of the first two albums? Touring with the likes of Bring Me The Horizon and The Ghost Inside The Van had a huge impact on You Me At Six. Heavier styles of music is something the band wanted to use on their own material. As they've gotten older their musical tastes have broadened and they're no longer restricted by their youth.

They didn't want to make the same album over and over again because it would be like cheating themselves as well as their fans. Progression is the word. Their aim was to prove to the media, and indeed their fans to an extent, that they are not a one trick pony. Even before their collaboration with Chiddy Bang or even their first album, You Me At Six were interested in different flavours of music and found fun ways of trying out new sounds in the studio. With their new album they wanted to be taken out of the teen-friendly pop-punk scene, quite literally. It was time for them to move on. They wanted to go into Foo Fighters territory; it's rock music that's accessible to a broad spectrum of music fans. It's rock music for the masses but still with enough kick to please their long-term fans. It was important for You Me At Six to reach a new audience.

The anticipated third album saw the band deliver a nifty marketing campaign. The official website had a five day timer with various changing images and details on their forthcoming studio album and when the timer reached its limit the album's artwork was revealed along with its tracklisting and title. Thousands of fans checked the website every day for news on the upcoming album. To promote the release, the band played four free in-store signings and performances at HMV stores in London, Manchester, Birmingham and Glasgow.

The band's third full-length studio opus was already causing quite a stir with the band's rapidly growing fanbase as pre-sales were growing exceedingly high and UK on-line retailers like Play.com were noticing an increase of interest in the band. Franceschi tweeted on August 3, 2011 that their third album had the

Performing at HMV for the album launch

Photo courtesy of Hugh Thompson/Rex Features

highest presales of any album in the history of Play.com.

In August, the band filmed a music video for the upcoming single 'Loverboy', before the album *Sinners Never Sleep* was released on October 3, 2011. Reaching Number 3 in the UK, this amazing chart success had cemented You Me At Six's position as one of British rock's biggest new acts.

> *"You Me At Six had cemented their position as one of British rock's brightest hopes."*

The album had a staggered international release: it came out in Australia and New Zealand on October 3 and in the USA on January 24, 2012. It hit Number 28 in Australia and Number 26 in Ireland. It seems fairly common these days for labels to issue albums in foreign countries over a period of time rather than release them simultaneously. It is a good way for both the label and artist to drum up extended support and gain further promotion.

The band were ecstatic with the response, both critically and commercially, which they got for the new album; to be in the charts with the likes of Adele, James Morrison and Lady Gaga proved that rock music was and is emphatically not dead. It seemed like You Me At Six were accomplishing everything they set out to do: they wanted to be in a band, have hit albums and maximise the opportunity to tour.

A deluxe edition of the album was issued featuring a documentary on the making of *Sinners Never Sleep* entitled *Bite My Tongue,* which highlighted the band's growing popularity. Dan Flint spoke to Dan Shields at *Soundsphere Mag*: "We've had people come down and film shows and we've recorded interviews two or three times, but it just wasn't very organised; this time, we knew we were going to LA to record the album, so we turned to the label and told them we wanted to film a documentary."

It is a heartfelt documentary showing how the band feels about their success and where they'd come from in the past five years. As with any band there's more than one personality and at times there is conflict and *Bite My Tongue* shows how the band deals with life in YMAS. The film was directed by Tim Matthia who was also behind the music video for 'Loverboy'. In the documentary each member is given chance to offer their own perspective on life in You Me At Six.

Chris Miller even made some critical comments about their first album *Take Off Your Colours*, which they made when they were teenagers. "I don't hate it," Franceschi concurred to Ed Cooper of the UK newspaper *The Independent*, "I don't think it's a bad album, I just don't think it's what we're about now; and I think that can be said about a lot of bands, you know."

The documentary represented both the closing of a chapter and the opening of a new era simply because they'd changed so much as a band and as people; in essence they'd grown up. *Sinners Never Sleep* was their first straight forward rock album and offered a new future for the band.

The band were thrilled with the knowledge that their third album had sold almost 30,000 copies in its first week of release and that fans had quickly latched on to songs like 'Bite My Tongue'. As with *Hold Me Down*, *Sinners Never Sleep* later went Silver, earning sales of over 60,000.

The album spawned the singles 'Loverboy' which hit Number 39 in the UK and Number 31 in the separate Scottish singles chart; 'Bite My Tongue', their collaboration with Oli Sykes, peaked at Number 124 and 'No One Does It Better' was released as the album's third single (though fans initially expected 'Jaws On The Floor' to be released given that the band had revealed artwork for it).

The initial video shoot for 'Loverboy' had to be delayed because of the London Riots; it was eventually aired on the band's YouTube channel on August 28. The band were very pleased with 'Loverboy' and felt it best represented the edgier rock sound of the album, confirming the progression; after the collaborative single 'Rescue Me', You Me At Six wanted fans to know that their new music definitely rocked in capital letters.

"I always check out YouTube comments," Max Helyer told Lewis Corner of *Digital Spy*. "It's always nice to see different people's perspectives. Some people say it's the best thing ever and that they're glad we've moved on from the Chiddy Bang stuff, whereas others are like 'This is not as good as their previous stuff.'"

The music video for 'Loverboy' has a premise where the band get arrested and questioned by police for simply for being a band. The clip showed yet again that the band were using all forms of what is referred to as 'New Media' to promote their music.

The music video for the band's collaboration with Oli Sykes 'Bite My Tongue' was first aired on YouTube on November 6, 2011, also directed by Tim Matthia who had since become a friend of the band as well as a trusted collaborator. "We got a really good connection with him," Helyer said about Matthia to *Straight Up Random*, "so he understood where we wanted to go with this song, and how we wanted it to look."

> *"I always check out YouTube comments. It's always nice to see different people's perspectives."*

They had a good time shooting the video over in the States and felt as though the quality of filming was superior in the USA than it is back home in England. It was a different type of music video that fans had come to expect from You Me At Six but the reception was positive and the band felt it was amongst their best work to date.

The singles releases also gave the band a chance to release some new material as B-sides that had previously not seen the light of day: 'Just Forget' was recorded during the *Sinners Never Sleep* sessions in 2010 while 'Brother' and 'Moonchild' were recorded back when *Hold Me Down* was made, while 'Retain', 'Over Us' and 'Your Birthday' were new tracks that had been excluded from the album. The 'Bite My Tongue' singles release provided an opportunity for the band to offer differing B-sides, namely their live covers of Foo Fighters songs for a 'Foo Fighters Medley'; they chose to cover 'All My Life', 'Bridge Burning' and 'Best Of You'. It was recorded on September 22 during a live session for Radio One.

Reviews of *Sinners Never Sleep* were much better than *Hold Me Down*. Alistair Lawrence wrote on *BBC Music*: "Looking to the future and into the past at the same time, *Sinners Never Sleep* is destined to sound a bit like a (frequently awkward) transition. Still, for a record that could've gone in one of two directions, it manages the neat trick of going in both."

Awarding the album 7/10, Gareth O'Malley wrote on the music, style and culture website *DIY*: "Maturity was never the issue for YM@6, [*sic*] though; there's a difference between making a conscious effort to 'grow up' and simply pushing things forward. The band have done the latter, and by their standards this is a wildly ambitious move."

Zach Redrup wrote in *Deadpress* that "With *Sinners Never Sleep*, You Me At Six have gone and matured into the band they aspired to be in their previous effort. Everything sounds more determined, some tracks sound almost anthemic, and they've wandered into places darker than they would've dared tread into before."

Tim Larsen wrote a positive 8/10 review on *Rockfreaks* and enthused: "Overall I think *Sinners Never Sleep* is a step in the right direction for a band whose initial hype is dying down, and who need to put out solid records like this to prove that they're in business for the long haul. YMAS prove that they can write the hooks that are so crucial for the genre just as consistently as ever…"

"This is a top notch release with great song after great song."

"This is a top notch release with great song after great song," said Ryan Williford on *Audio Opinions*. "Even when the band goes into ballad mode on 'Crash', it turns out to be an amazing and emotional song." There were the odd dissenters: Mischa Pearlman wrote on *Thrash Hits*: "The problem, it seems, is that You Me At Six are uncertain which direction to move in. As a result they've made an album that flirts between who they were and who they want to be, but not one that really demonstrates who they actually are."

"We were all quite surprised," Matt Barnes said to Sam Panasuik at *Leeds Music Scene*. "We never knew

116

it would have this good of a reception. I thought some people were gonna hate it and some people were gonna love it."

It was time to hit the road again. The band started to tour almost as soon as the album had come out and fans quickly warmed to the new material. It was important to the band to spend at least the next twelve months touring around the world making sure their album was available in as many territories as possible and generally building up a fanbase outside of their native UK. Therefore America, Asia, Australia and, of course the UK were all on the touring agenda for 2011 and beyond.

You Me At Six journeyed to the other side of the world for a tour with The Mission In Motion and We The Kings in Australia. "We love playing our songs with our fans knowing all the words and singing along," Matt Barnes said to *Rock Kent* at the time of the album's release. "I'm really looking forward to playing 'Bite My Tongue' or 'Time Is Money' live!"

They'd only done one headlining tour of Australia in the past and had taken part in the increasingly popular Soundwave tour so it was important for the band to let their Australian fans know that they hadn't forgotten about them before the new album came out Down Under.

You Me At Six try to keep their live shows as consistent as possible so as not to let their hardened fans down. They are a band that feeds directly off the audience and have a great rapport with them, which makes the shows work so well, especially in the band's native UK. They could play a great show to thousands of people in one country and give an equally top-notch performance to a tiny crowd of a hundred people in another country, such is their dedication to improving themselves as a live band. It is exactly the right mentality to have during life on the road.

They had a great time touring with The Mission In Motion and We The Kings because all three bands are "fans bands" in the sense that they have strong ties with their fans and spend time doing meet-and-greets and chatting backstage and outside the venues. They also get on well with one another and had time to hang out and even watch each other perform onstage on some nights. You Me At Six had also gained a great deal of press coverage Down Under. Tahila Pitchford reviewed The Roundhouse gig in Sydney for *The AU Review* and enthused: "Finally it was You Me At Six's turn to rock out The Roundhouse, and that is exactly what they did. Blowing all other competition out of the water, the British boys proved just why they are one of the most exciting live bands to see right now. Opening on 'The Consequence', the energy was high from the get-go, with the crowd singing along almost as loudly as lead singer Josh Franceschi."

Reviewing the final night at the Fowler's Live in Adelaide, a writer for *FasterLouder* enthused: "Lead singer Josh Franceschi is full of energy, running around on stage, reminiscent of the on-stage presence of Paramore singer Hayley Williams. No matter how big or small the stage, Josh made it his own."

On tour in Australia the band also had a taste of what it is like for bands to struggle with government politics in various countries. Due to alcohol licensing laws and because of the venues they were playing in, it was not possible to play to all of their fans, many of whom were under eighteen years of age. You Me At Six know how to support their teenage fans and were not going to let anyone down; they wanted to have the opportunity to be able to play to anyone who wanted to see them so they managed to get around the situation. "We're not coming all the way out to Australia to let people down," Franceschi told *Bombshell Zine*, "and people want to come and see us, and we need to make that available. Regardless of the amount of people, we need to make it that whoever wants to be catered for, can be catered for. In the end, we fought so much that we got it. We did an U18 and 18+ show in Brisbane, and also an acoustic instore, and what was strange was that there were more people of all ages at the instore than there were at the show because it was more convenient."

The band believed they had created a stronger set of songs on their third album and wanted to concentrate on new material rather than songs from its two predecessors. However, it is inevitable that some quarters of the band's fanbase would want to hear the older songs despite the band's preferences.

Obviously the worst part of being on tour for any band is that fact that they are away from their family and friends. "Before we go on the road we like to spend as much time at home with our friends and families, as we are obviously not going to see them for a while," Dan Flint admitted to *The Sound Alarm*'s Bekka Collins. "Life can be quite hectic on tour so most nights we all just chill at home and maybe play some Xbox!"

Between October 8 and October 15 the band played a sold-out tour of the UK starting in Preston at The 53 Degrees and winding up in London at Brixton Academy. It was the band's first UK tour in about seven months and they were excited to be back on the road on their home turf and playing smaller venues this time too. They wanted to feel more like a band and so playing in cosier venues with modest production facilities gave them the opportunity to do that. The band's mentality at the time was that it's a good thing to play in different sized venues; playing big arenas all the time creates egos but travelling to places to like Middlesbrough and Preston gave the band a chance to stay in touch with their club roots whilst also maintaining a tight rapport with their fans. You Me At Six adore both the big production values and intensity of a festival performance as well as the intimacy and sweat-induced claustrophobia of a club show.

By this point the band had their own tour bus which made a change from the early days when they used to travel to gigs via public transport. They're lucky to have the kind of success that has afforded them a crew and transport facilities but they've worked hard to earn it.

"Before we go on the road we like to spend as much time at home with our friends and families."

Back in December 2010 Dan Flint spoke to Scott Williams of *eGigs* about the band's desire to play the more localised areas of the country rather than just obvious cities like Manchester and London. "In the UK we usually only get to go on a tour of the major cities," he said, "and that means it can be done in only a week or a week and a half. We really want to hit up every town we've not played before."

This time the band took Lower Than Atlantis and Deaf Havana on the road with them as support acts. It was a strong bill and the three bands bounced off each other and attracted some great reviews from the UK press.

"When the music kicked off, You Me At Six proved that they were worth their salt," penned Cat Marr in *The Leeds Guide* of the band's performance at the Leeds O2 Academy on October 12. "They were focused and rhythmically tight, stopping for frequent minor guitar and drum solos, this showed that their hearts still belongs to their instruments."

Reviewing the band's gig at the Southampton Guildhall on October 13, Ed Cooper wrote in *Hit The Floor Magazine*: "Frontman Franceschi proved his worth by tackling the heavier vocals of 'Bite My Tongue' – a verse in which friend Oliver Sykes sang on the record. It is a rare moment where a band sounds near enough exactly how they do on the record and the set in Southampton was one of these moments."

Obviously they wanted to play some of their new stuff because they had an album to promote but they were also happy to play their older material. A number of the songs from *Take Off Your Colours* were not reflective of where the band were now at. However, they didn't want to drop everything out of the set-list from that album. They once saw Finch live and were disappointed not to hear 'Letters To You' so You Me At Six are aware that some fans do want to hear the older stuff. There were certain songs, however, from the first album such as 'Gossip' which the band have simply moved on from. "We've got to move on from that stuff," Franceschi said to Tom Goodwyn at *NME*. "People ask us now why we don't play it live and it's because it's the shittest song in existence."

You Me At Six's set-list on this tour usually consisted of: 'The Consequence', 'Jaws On The Floor', 'Safer To Hate Her', 'Save It For The Bedroom', 'Liquid Confidence', 'Trophy Eyes', 'Contagious Chemistry', 'Bite My Tongue', 'Playing The Blame Game', 'Fireworks', 'Little Death', 'Tigers And Sharks', 'Loverboy', 'Stay With Me' and 'Underdog'.

"We get a lot of chips and dips: Doritos, Monster Munch, Mini Cheddars, a bit of chocolate, a bit of fruit that no-one ever eats," Dan Flint said to Joe Hawkes of *The Edge* when asked about the band's tour rider. "Obviously beer, cider, vodka, a bit of rum."

The band then excitedly committed themselves to a headlining tour of the USA in October, which was one of 2011's highlights. Getting the chance to journey around America again was not something they wanted to turn down. They had some new music to promote and wanted to play the new tracks to their American fans as well as maybe picking up new fans too.

The band took part in a couple of celebratory shows during this period too; the first was a 25th Anniversary show to celebrate *Q* magazine as part of their 'Live At Concrete' series. Tickets were free for the East London gig on November 28. They played 'The Consequence', 'Jaws On The Floor', 'Safer To Hate Her', 'Liquid Confidence', 'No One Does It Better', 'Chemistry', 'Bite My Tongue', 'Fireworks', 'Little Death', 'Lover Boy', 'Stay With Me' and 'Underdog'.

Joe Bishop wrote on *Q* magazine's website: "Playing a set that mixed slow and fast songs, the show culminating in a highly energetic rendition of fan-favourite 'Underdog', during which the band leapt off stage, walked to the bar and ordered a round of tequila shots, which they downed before heading back to blitz out the final chorus." On December 13, the band then took part in the 40th Anniversary celebrations of the iconic Hard Rock Café by playing an exclusive show hosted by Absolute Radio.

You Me At Six still enjoyed listening to other bands and going to see them live; they found time to watch Enter Shikari (a band they'd supported in the past), in Manchester earlier in the year. "I think there is a lot of British talent out there at the moment," Matt Barnes told Sam Panasuik of *Leeds Music Scene*. "We saw Enter Shikari the other night and they were incredible... I reckon they have a good chance of getting it this year but if we could hold down the fort that would be insane." They even had time to see Jimmy Eat World and Foo Fighters, which they relished.

The band members usually try to hang out and meet their fans but it's not always possible especially as the crowds are getting bigger by the year. They have meet-and-greets at the bigger UK venues and at the smaller venues they usually wait around the venue, chatting with fans and signing autographs.

As the world has entered a digital age when products such as CDs and DVDs are being replaced by on-line files, bands know that the main way to make money is to tour and sell merchandise on the road. There's far less no money to be made from selling CDs unless, of course, sales are literally in the millions. Fans would often rather go and watch a band play live.

"I'm a massive CD collector, it would be a shame if everything just went digital now," Max Helyer told *Air3 Radio*. "I like to have a hard copy of something so when I grow up I've got something I can look back on; with digital, if your computer breaks or you forget your password then all the music you did buy you can't have."

In late 2011 the band had spoken about plans to tour parts of Southeast Asia to promote the album, such as Singapore, Japan, Malaysia and Indonesia as well as Europe in 2012. Playing at festivals like Reading and Leeds had previously provided awe-inspiring moments for the band but to travel to such remote countries was like a dream come true for them. They yearned to travel to places that they'd never been to before and that are not often frequented by rock bands from the Western World.

"We get a lot of chips and dips: Doritos, Monster Munch, Mini Cheddars, a bit of chocolate, a bit of fruit that no-one ever eats."

They also announced that they would again take part in the annual summer touring festival of the USA, the Vans Warped Tour 2012. "When you're there it's a tough thing," Helyer confessed to *Straight Up Random* in 2011. "It is a gruelling tour, it's not the easiest of tours, but then you do look back and reflect on it and go, 'We had a really good time this summer doing what we want to do, having a good laugh with a lot of good people, and actually playing music to kids that like music,' you know?"

The band's relationship with their fans remains remarkably close
Photo courtesy of Hugh Thompson/Rex Features

Touring the USA is an expensive endeavour but the Vans Warped Tour was the perfect way for You Me At Six and other low-key and up-and-coming bands to make their name known to American rock and punk fans.

"They really do make you work hard on the Warped Tour," Helyer admitted to Steve O'Gallagher of *Push To Fire* in 2010. "You have to get up at like 7a.m. to find out what time your band's playing and you have to get all the merch tents set up and all your gear ready, and you can be dragging gear across a dusty car park for like a mile."

Like any band, however, You Me At Six want to make a splash on the influential American market and *Sinners Never Sleep* was a good enough album to prove their worth. A great number of British bands head across the Atlantic with the wrong intentions; some bands that want to break America expect everything to fall in to place as soon as they set foot in New York or LA. It's not always the case. You Me At Six knew from the time they first went to the USA that they had to connect with American fans; make them aware that their music is worth listening to. They knew that if they could attract the attention of American kids wearing Paramore and Jimmy Eat World T-shirts, then they'd have the chance of making some new fans in the States.

You Me At Six feel that British audiences are crazy; often jumping around, screaming, singing to the songs and having fun even if they don't know the band's music all that well. "But in America you have to try a lot harder to get them to do anything," Chris Miller admitted to Megan White of *Counteract Magazine*. "It's still great fun, it's nice having a new challenge and being able to play for different people. But it's amazing, I love touring there, it's good fun."

You Me At Six have a strong work ethic and a principled approach to the music world. However, it's good to let loose every once in a while which is what the band did when they finished a previous UK tour in Yeovil. "We went to a club and partied, then got a [hotel]," Flint told Amber Tan of *Purple Revolver*. "We persuaded the support bands to come too. There were about fifteen of us in two rooms. We partied and paid for it all in cash. We pretty much trashed the room, a foot went through the wall, people were in the shower. We didn't get kicked out and the bar person even came up and partied with us."

"We never started the band to get famous or rich," Dan Flint admitted to Tyler of *Neck Deep Media*. "We all started it because we wanted to be in a band. If you're in it for the money and fame, then you're in it for the wrong reasons. But if you're lucky enough to get rich and famous as a successful band, then you should really appreciate that."

Away from the stage, the band had embarked on some personal endeavours that – on the surface – don't appear to be particularly rock 'n' roll. In mid-2011, rhythm guitarist Max Helyer founded his own clothes line called 'Become Antique'. Helyer had followed in the footsteps of bassist Matt Barnes who had moved into the world of fashion and formed his own clothes line back in late 2007. He named his brand 'Cheer Up! Clothing' and enjoyed the support of some famous rock star artists to champion his company, namely members of The All-American Rejects, VersaEmerge, We Are In The Crowd, Four Year Strong and Emarosa.

Singer Josh Franceschi also started his own clothing company too called 'Down But Not Out'. Asked by blogger Darryl Smyers of the *Dallas Observer* if his new clothing line takes up a lot of his spare time, Franceschi admitted: "Yes, but the typical day is handled by my dad and my best friend. I can use email if I get an idea. It's a lovely relationship. It's a very rewarding thing. People have taken a notice to what we are doing. It's fun."

Are we seeing a theme here? The band had wanted to express themselves individually outside of the world of music and having an interest in fashion they opted to create their own clothing brands.

"Being creative people, you don't always want to focus on music," Dan Flint told Joe Hawkes of *The Edge* about his bandmates endeavours into the world of fashion. "When they're on tour they can get away from the You Me At Six stuff, and you can really focus your energy on something else, which I think is always key to not going insane on tour."

Their other hobbies include playing video games (usually on the Xbox) although not everyone in the band enjoys the sports games, particularly football. "FIFA sucks, FIFA is so boring," Matt Barnes confessed to Claire White of *Flecking Records*. "I don't play football games and I hate football, and I hate sport to be honest. But I put on FIFA and I was like 'Right!', I was the best team, I was Chelsea then I was playing some team in Austria that was like a local team, and they had like one star and really bad stats. On the easiest setting it was still one-all so I tackled in their penalty box, then they scored a penalty and I managed to just score one goal so… I hate that game."

"It's a very rewarding thing. People have taken a notice to what we are doing. It's fun."

2011 was another great – albeit exhausting! – year for the band given the success of *Sinners Never Sleep* and the constant touring which hugely publicised their name around the world. They also won 'Best British Band' at the *Kerrang! Awards* after losing out each time to Bullet For My Valentine in 2008, 2009 and 2010. It was natural for them to feel as though they'd deserved to win the award after losing out in the past. "We were on the same table as [Bullet For My Valentine] at the awards and we really thought they were gonna win it again," Matt Barnes said to *Rock Kent*: "When they announced that we won we were so shocked! I would love to watch our reaction to winning that year but unfortunately they didn't film it this year!"

"There was a little bit of banter but honestly all of those bands would have deserved the award, so I think everyone was just happy to be in the running for it," Dan Flint admitted to Gena Hollyoake at *News Beat Media*. Certainly winning 'Best British Band' was as good as winning, say, 'Best Album' or 'Best Live Band'. You Me At Six were finally getting the recognition they deserved.

The timing could not have been better too, given the low-points the band sunk to after the unexpected cancellation of the Blink-182 tour, so winning 'Best British Band' certainly helped build morale within the camp. "We haven't really done anything, we were recording the album which is a high point for us, but there was so much stress around it," Franceschi admitted to *Bombshell Zine*, "the Blink thing, the Parkway tour, we've all had stuff going on, and then we won 'Best British Band' and we were just like 'Holy shit!' We can't believe we won this award, so it was a massive pick me up and it really was quite special."

Moving into the New Year, the band committed themselves to a tour of Indonesia playing four dates in Jakarta, Surabaya, Yogyakarta and Bali. Coming from a leafy and affluent town outside of London, the band were totally psyched about playing in parts of the world that they'd maybe never even imagined visiting. Back on the road then. "One minute you think you have a month at home, the next day you get a call saying that you have been offered a tour [and] you'll be on the road for two months," Chris Miller explained to *SCAN*'s Conor Scrivener. "But it's what I've always wanted to do, so it's worth it in the end, especially when you think of the bright side."

To promote the January 2012 release of *Sinners Never Sleep* in the USA, the band went on the road as headliners for the first time in that country, with The Swellers, Twin Atlantic and We Are The Ocean in support (all British bands aside from The Swellers). "That was a completely conscious decision," Franceschi admitted to Shane Richardson of *Alternative Press*. "We went through the tour submissions from other bands, but we decided that we wanted to tour with our friends."

The tour kicked off on January 24 in Ohio and finished at The Troubadour in LA on February 14. "This is our first ever 'tour' in America where we are doing it by bus," Franceschi told Tyler of *Neck Deep Media*. "We did the logistics and it's only like $100 extra to be in a bus than doing vans and hotels, so we were obviously like, 'We're getting that bus.'"

You Me At Six loved touring America; a country where so many British bands have made major impressions from The Beatles to Radiohead. It is such a large country with a saturated music industry that bands have to work extra hard to get a foothold. It's still about playing as many shows as possible, as well as possible and gathering a fanbase over time. There is no quick fix. They were lucky that *Sinners Never Sleep* had been given positive reviews by their fans and many music journalists Stateside. They had something good to promote; something to be proud of. America is certainly on the horizon for future tours. What YMAS adore about America is what most British bands love: the weather, the beaches, the culture and the relaxed way of life in certain US cities. It's the other side of the Atlantic, far away from home.

"We can't believe we won this award, so it was a massive pick me up and it really was quite special."

Selma Rakovic reviewed the band's gig at The Palladium in Worcester, Massachusetts for *The Inspirer*: "It was clear that You Me At Six would be the star of the night's show. With deafening screams, the crowd, composed of an overwhelming number of girls, welcomed the Brits who immediately proceeded to bounce around the stage in their signature fashion. Man, have things changed since I first saw them in 2008, I thought, and I was soon shoved aside by a pack of eager teenage girls screaming 'Josh, I love you!' You Me At Six focused mostly on songs from *Sinners Never Sleep*…"

The band had worked very hard back home in the

UK and had spent years building up a fanbase but it is going to be just as much hard work – if not harder – to translate such a following over to the United States. There is still an awful lot of work to do before they break America but they are committed to making it happen.

> ## *"It was clear that You Me At Six would be the star of the night's show."*

Following on from the USA tour, they ventured to Australia, another favourite country of theirs, as part of Soundwave Festival Tour as well as performing shows on their own with The Used and A Day To Remember. The Soundwave Festival included System Of A Down, Slipknot, Limp Bizkit and Marilyn Manson with dates in Brisbane, Sydney, Melbourne, Adelaide and Perth between February 25 and March 5. By now, Australian audiences had really warmed to the British band.

Helyer spoke enthusiastically to *I Like Music* about the band's final night in Perth: "We're ending a great day, we've all sunk a few lagers and we're having a good time so far. Going to go watch a bit of Slipknot and System Of A Down, then celebrate my birthday when it hits twelve o'clock tonight at the after-party! It's going to be a right good laugh."

Perhaps the Australian live music scene is not as thriving as it is in the UK and USA so when bands do tour Australia they get a fantastic response all over the country. Australian music fans have treated You Me At Six really well and the atmosphere at a You Me At Six gig Down Under is a memorable experience for the band and the crowds they attract. Australia is a country that You Me At Six definitely want to continue to tour so long as the fans over there want them to. Yet again the band were picking up positive reviews from critics outside of their native Britain.

"We're ending a great day, we've all sunk a few lagers and we're having a good time so far."

Reviewing You Me At Six as well as A Day To Remember and The Used at the UNSW Roundhouse in Sydney on February 28, Poppy Reid wrote on *The Music Network*: "Pausing for every 'bitch' and 'shit' [in Josh's between song banter] wasn't the only reminder it was an all-ages event. One sweet young man stopped to text his mum after the heart-wrenching 'Jaws On The Floor'. The requested crowd surfers for 'Dilemma' started a consistent spilling over the barrier; a constant which later clocked up over 200 bodies for security, according to one guard."

For many of these shows, You Me At Six's set-list was: 'The Consequence', 'Kiss And Tell', 'Save It For The Bedroom', 'Playing The Blame Game', 'Loverboy', 'Safer To Hate Her', 'Trophy Eyes', 'If I

Were In Your Shoes', 'Fireworks', 'Liquid Confidence', 'Stay With Me' and 'Underdog'.

Although You Me At Six may seem like a seasoned band given the wealth of experience they have gained since 2007, there are still tricks of the trade they enjoy learning and they're not daft enough to assume they know everything. "One thing we learnt on one of our first big tours was from a band called The Sleeping, they said if you don't come off stage sweating, then you haven't worked hard enough that night in your performance," said Max Helyer to Danni Davies at *Resonace UK*. "Still to this day when I play I think of those things they have said and put every bit of energy I have into our live performance. If you have seen us then I'm sure you can see it."

Back home, the band played a lengthy tour of the UK in March and April with Kids In Glass Houses at such venues as Manchester Apollo, London's Brixton Academy, Nottingham Rock City and Liverpool University. Having not played in the UK since October the band were psyched about returning to British shores for a hefty bout of shows scattered all over the country. Many dates were sold-out in advance and cities such as Manchester and London saw second dates added. "But in mainland Europe we're still at the four to seven hundred market in terms of capacity," Franceschi told *The Independent*'s Ed Cooper. "We're still building internationally, so we can go off and play smaller shows, then come back to the UK and do a sell-out tour."

Surely stadium shows beckon?
Photo courtesy of Nathan Dainty/Rex Features

However, the Belfast and Dublin dates had to be rescheduled to April 7 and April 8, respectively, due to Franceschi's tonsillitis. In the two Irish cities, You Me At Six were supported by Mayday Parade and The Skints. 'Underdog' and 'Stay With Me' are probably the songs that best represent the band and where they are at this stage in their career. They're muscular, catchy and powerful rock songs that are near-permanent fixtures in the band's set-lists and proof that over the years the band have grown more accustomed at crafting a balanced and climatic set-list.

They also performed at the famed rock and metal event Download Festival at Castle Donington on June 9, which was another great day for them. At the time of writing, 2012 has shaped up to be another busy year of touring for the band but touring is not something they're afraid of, simply because they know it will make them a better, more experienced and tight outfit. They just wanted to make sure their new album is heard by as many people as possible.

The band were given a couple of exciting opportunities in 2012 that could potentially broaden their fanbase. They hooked up with Thorpe Park in Surrey to help promote one of the new attractions called 'The Swarm', which received massive media publicity. "That's the newest thing that we've written," Helyer told *I Like Music* about the band's single, also called 'The Swarm', "and it comes out on the March 18, with the ride opening on March 15.

Basically, we got to sit down with Thorpe Park, who chose us as the first band in the world ever to write a song for a theme park! We were really stoked for that. The ride has a 127-feet drop at the start and is Europe's tallest winged rollercoaster!"

Also, You Me At Six were named Future Flame Ambassadors for the 2012 London Olympics. Organised by Coca-Cola, Future Flame Ambassadors gives the chance for young people aged sixteen to

> *"Still to this day when I play I think of those things they have said and put every bit of energy I have into our live performance. If you have seen us then I'm sure you can see it."*

twenty five to carry the Olympic Torch. It's a positive step for the younger generation of the country at a time when British youths have a somewhat negative image after the London Riots of 2011, and youth unemployment is disturbingly high. Much of You Me At Six's fanbase is teenage so they have the target audience for the event.

Guitarist Chris Miller said to Conor Scrivener of *SCAN*: "It's basically a program that was offered to us and with the Olympics coming to the UK it's a massive deal, something we are probably never going to see in our lifetime again, so having the opportunity to get involved and do stuff for it was really exciting and we took it up instantly."

As Future Flame Ambassadors, it gives the chosen artists and athletes the opportunity to work with young people from diverse backgrounds. The band were pleased that they had been given a chance to be role models for young people and to be part of such an awe-inspiring event.

There are yet more aims to accomplish, of course: perhaps a Number 1 album in the UK and USA would be high up on the list for any band as well as headlining a gig at Wembley Arena or even Wembley Stadium?; performing in the top three slot at Reading and Leeds Festival and playing on the Main Stage at a festival like the Vans Warped Tour perhaps?! Maybe one day You Me At Six will found their own record label? They've managed to stay grounded and rational but they still harbour an abundance of enthusiasm.

With yet more bursts of heavy touring around the world planned for 2012 and beyond, and of course another album in the works too, You Me At Six are set to be one of Britain's most high-profile and consistently popular bands. They have a growing fanbase and have finally entered the mainstream consciousness with *Sinners Never Sleep*. Where will they go with their next album? What direction will they take? They'd certainly opened up new avenues for themselves after *Sinners Never Sleep*.

Nominated for five awards at the 2012 annual

Kerrang! Awards in London, You Me At Six picked up 'Best British Band' at a ceremony that saw metal stalwarts Black Sabbath pick up the 'Inspiration Award'. Speaking to BBC Newsbeat, Chris Miller enthused: "It's crazy. We've all grown up with *Kerrang!* since before we could play guitars. We always got our musical knowledge from it – so this is awesome."

Three albums in six years plus the constant touring has proven that You Me At Six are not afraid of hard work. They never seem to get a spare moment and are constantly writing new material or playing a show or doing an interview. Franceschi told *Straight Up Random*: "I mean, we haven't really stopped since we started to be honest. It's always been exciting to write new records and the music. I don't think it's the same as it was before where a band could release a record, and tour it non-stop for eighteen months, and then go, 'Okay, let's write another one.'"

It became evident around the time of the band's acclaimed debut release that they were going to be something special and that their strict work ethic was going to pay off. You Me At Six appear to have made a fairly hefty dent in several foreign markets where they play to several hundred people at each gig and sell thousands of albums. They knew at an early stage that it was important to remain level-headed and that's what they were going to do. They have shown confidence but not arrogance in their abilities as a band. You Me At Six could be filling stadiums in the next few years and having Number 1 albums all around the world. They know that it is a step-by-step process and that patience not greed is a virtue.

They are doing something they've dreamed of doing since they formed the band; they want to continue to travel around the world, see new places, make new fans and build up their reputation as a hard-working

> *"It's crazy. We've all grown up with Kerrang! since before we could play guitars."*

live band. "Our main goal," Chris Miller confessed to *SCAN*'s Conor Scrivener, "has always just been to be a band for as long as we possibly can and to keep making albums and CDs as that's what we enjoy doing, writing songs and sharing it with people."

Always a band to look ahead rather than behind, the origins of the group are firmly left in the past as You Me At Six concentrate on their future ambitions. "I was only sixteen," singer Josh Franceschi said to Danni Murphy of *The White Haven Guide*, "but I was singing when I was fifteen then I left school and I went to college and joined a band. *Kerrang!* wrote an article about us and it was the biggest thing in the world at the time and I've never looked back really."

Perseverance is the key word in the band's camp. They've worked hard in the past and continue to work even harder and have gone out there and met people in their efforts to build up a whole network of contacts to promote their music. Being in a band is not the easiest job in the world. Of course it can also be a great deal of fun and very glamorous at times too but it can still be very disconcerting and difficult. You Me At Six are dedicated to the band and at improving themselves as musicians too. These guys have their heads screwed on.

The future is looking good for You Me At Six...

Discography

ALBUMS

Take Off Your Colours:
The Truth Is A Terrible Thing/Gossip/Call That A Comeback?/Jealous Minds Think Alike/Save It For The Bedroom/Take Off Your Colours/You've Made Your Bed (So Sleep In It)/If You Run/Tigers And Sharks/If I Were In Your Shoes/Always Attract/Nasty Habits/The Rumour
CD – Slam Dunk/Epitaph 2008

Hold Me Down:
The Consequence/Underdog/Playing The Blame Game/Stay With Me/Safer To Hate Her/Take Your Breath Away/Liquid Confidence (Nothing To Lose)/Hard To Swallow/Contagious Chemistry/There's No Such Thing As Accidental Infidelity/Trophy Eyes/Fireworks/Fact-tastic
CD – Virgin 2010

Sinners Never Sleep:
Loverboy/Jaws On The Floor/Bite My Tongue/This Is The First Thing/No One Does It Better/Little Death/Crash/Reckless/Time Is Money/Little Bit Of Truth/The Dilemma/When We Were Younger
CD – Virgin 2011

EPs

We Know What It Means To Be Alone:
Promise, Promise/New Jersey/This Turbulence Is Beautiful/Taste/The Liar And The Lighter
CD/Download – Independent 2006

Untitled:
The Rumour/Gossip/Noises/This Turbulence Is Beautiful
CD/Download – Independent 2006

SINGLES

Save It For The Bedroom (2007)

If I Were In Your Shoes (2008)
Gossip (2008)
Jealous Minds Think Alike (2008)

Finders Keepers (2009)
Kiss And Tell (2009)

Underdog (2010)
Liquid Confidence (2010)
Stay With Me (2010)
Starry Eyed (2010)

Rescue Me (2011)
Loverboy (2011)
Bite My Tongue (2011)
Knew It Was You (2011)

Takes One To Know One (2011)

No One Does It Better (2012)

MUSIC VIDEOS

Save It For The Bedroom
Dir: Lawrence Hardy, 2007

If I Were In Your Shoes
Dir: Lawrence Hardy, 2008

Gossip
Dir: Greg Allan, 2008

Jealous Minds Think Alike
Dir: Shane Davey, 2008

Save It For The Bedroom (Reissue)
Dir: Shane Davey, 2009

Finders Keeps
Dir: Nick Bartlett, 2009

Kiss And Tell
Dir: James Copeman, 2009

The Consequence
Dir: Lawrence Hardy, 2010

Underdog
Dir: Nick Bartlett, 2010

Liquid Confidence
Dir: Adam Powell, 2010

Stay With Me
Dir: Frank Borin, 2010

Rescue Me
Dir: James Lees, 2011

Loverboy
Dir: Eran Creevy, 2011

BIBLIOGRAPHY & SOURCES

The author would like to thank the following publications and websites, which were integral in researching this book:

MAGAZINES & NEWSPAPERS

The Guardian, The Independent, Kerrang!, Metro, NME, The Observer, Q, Rock Sound

WEBSITES

http://alternativemusichub.com
http://audioopinions.net
http://blogs.dallasobserver.com
http://blogs.independent.co.uk
http://changetherecord.net
http://counteract-magazine.com
http://designermagazine.tripod.com
http://grafwall.indiestar.t
http://hangout.altsounds.com
http://livethescene.com
http:// music.thedigitalfix.com
http://musicdune.com
http://news.bbc.co.uk
http://newbeatsmedia.com
http://pushtofire.com
http://rock-metal-punk.org
http://rushonrock.com
http://scan.lusu.co.uk
http://sputnikmusic.com
http://straightuprandom.com

http://strangeglue.com
http://thephoenix.com
http://thesoundalarm.com
http://thisisfakediy.co.uk
http://underthegunreview.net
http://withdrumsandcolour.com
http://www.air3radio.com
http://www.allmusic.com
http://www.allthingsnow.com
http://www.altpress.com
http://www.backstagepost.com
http://www.baeblemusic.com
http:// www.bbc.co.uk/music
http://www.bombshellzine.com
http://www.bringthenoise.co.uk
http://www.brumlive.com
http://www.caughtinthecrossfire.com
http://www.deadpress.co.uk
http://www.digitalspy.co.uk
http://www.drivenfaroff.com
http://www.egigs.co.uk
http:// www.entertainmentcardiff.com
http://www.eveningnews24.co.uk
http://www.fasterlouder.com.au
http://www.femalefirst.co.uk
http://www.fleckingrecords.co.uk
http://www.gigwise.com
http://www.hevypetal.com
http://www.hitlab.com
http://www.hitthefloor.co.uk
http://www.ilikemusic.com

http://www.indielondon.co.uk
http://www.inthenews.co.uk
http://www.theleedsguide.co.uk
http://www.leedsmusicscene.net
http://www.malextra.com
http://www.mikedolbear.com
http://www.mintsouth.com
http://www.neckdeepmedia.com
http://www.nme.com
http://www.noise11.com
http://www.noizemakesenemies.co.uk
http://www.ourzonemag.com
http://www.purplerevolver.com
http://www.resonanceuk.com
http://www.rockfreaks.net
http://www.rockkent.com
http://www.roomthirteen.com
http://www.scotsman.com
http://www.soundspheremag.com
http://www.strangeglue.com
http://www.streetnortheast.com
http://www.theaureview.com
http://www.theedgesusu.co.uk
http:// www.theinspirer.nu
http://www.themusicnetwork.com
http://www.thenewcurrent.com
http://www.theskinny.co.uk
http://www.thewhitehavenguide.co.uk
http://www.thrashhits.com
http://www.virgin.com
http://www.xfm.co.uk

ACKNOWLEDGEMENTS

Thank you to the following journalists for their excellent work covering the career of You Me At Six, which has proved hugely helpful in writing this book: Mark Ashby, Joe Barton, Lewis Bazley, Jason Birchmeier, Joe Bishop, Ben Brady, Steven Burnett, Andy Burton, George Cannings, Chloe Chaplin, Michael Christopher, Bekka Collins, Ed Cooper, Lewis Corner, Danni Davies, Kitty Empire, Jack Foley, Tom Goodwyn, Arwa Haider, Naomi Havergal, Joe Hawkes, Gena Hollyoake, Emma Jackson, Emma Johnston, Tim Larsen, Alistair Lawrence, Victoria Leggett, Joe Lennox, Cat Marr, Dee Massey, Ben Minsky, Michelle Moore, Danni Murphy, Lais MW, Tim Newbound, Steve O'Gallagher, Gareth O'Malley, Jamie Otsa, Sam Panasuik, Mischa Pearlman, Jeff Perkins, Tahila Pitchford, Simon Price, Selma Rakovic, Raziq Rauf, Zach Redup, Poppy Reid, Shane Richardson, Simon Rushworth, Chris Salmon, Conor Scrivener, Dan Shields, Darryl Smyers, Adam Spall, Amber Tan, Tyler, Tom Walsh, Claire White, Megan White, Scott Williams, Ryan Williford, Aidan Williamson and Hollie Witchalls. Thank you also to Martin Roach at Independent Music Press.

Thank you to the copyright holders for allowing the author to quote from the referenced sources/texts. However, it has not been entirely possible to contact every copyright holder though great efforts were made by the author. The author and publisher would be happy to amend/delete/credit, where appropriate, any sources in future editions of this work should the copyright holders get in touch. A special thank you must go to all those whose work the author has referenced in this book.

Also on Independent Music Press

www.impbooks.com

Also On Independent Music Press

PARAMORE
GRACE
by Ben Welch

The first and only biography of one of music's
biggest new rock acts. From prodigiously talented
teenagers to globe-trotting megastars, Paramore
have established themselves as one of the foremost
bands in mainstream rock music. However, with the
success has come the pressure of growing up
under the media's scrutiny, the demands of a
gruelling tour schedule and numerous line-up
changes. This test of character brought Paramore
to the brink of collapse. And yet from this adversity,
Paramore have returned with their most confident,
accomplished and deeply personal album to date –
Brand New Eyes. This is the first and only book to
tell their tale.

ISBN: 978-1-906191-16-0 Paperback, 144 Pgs
including 50 integrated colour pics, 230x170mm
World Rights £9.99